CONSTRUCTING INCEST STORIES

CONSTRUCTING INCEST STORIES

Black Women's Voices in Fact and Fiction

Dorothy L. Hurley
and
E. Anthony Hurley

Africa World Press, Inc.

| P.O. Box 1892 | | P.O. Box 48 |
| Trenton, NJ 08607 | | Asmara, ERITREA |

1-25-11

Africa World Press, Inc.

P.O. Box 1892
Trenton, NJ 08607

P.O. Box 48
Asmara, ERITREA

Book design: Saverance Publishing Services
Cover design: Ashraful Haque

Library of Congress Cataloging-in-Publication Data

Hurley, Dorothy L.
Constructing incest stories : black women's voices in fact and fiction / Dorothy L. Hurley and E. Anthony Hurley.
    p. cm.
Includes bibliographical references and index.
ISBN 1-59221-710-9 (cloth) -- ISBN 1-59221-711-7 (pbk.)
1. Incest--United States. 2. Incest victims--United States--Psychology. 3. Women, Black--United States. 4. Incest in literature. I. Hurley, E. Anthony. II. Title.

HV6570.7.H87 2009
306.877089'96073--dc22

                                    2009023002

Contents

Acknowledgments   vii

Introduction   1

I FACT

Chapter One – In Their Own Words   19

   Ashley's Story   22

   Gabrielle's Story   28

   Destiny's Story   33

   Kayla's Story   38

II FICTION

Chapter Two – Popularizing the Unspeakable: *I'm Telling*   45

Chapter Three – Fictionalizing the Clinical: *In My Bedroom*   63

Chapter Four – Incest in the Raw: *Push*   87

Chapter Five – Spiritualizing Incest: *The Color Purple*   117

Chapter Six – Disrupting the Text of Nature: *The Bluest Eye*   145

Afterword   169

References   173

Index   175

Acknowledgments

The women who bravely shared their stories for this book cannot be acknowledged by name. They are the resilient constructors of incest stories whose very telling saves lives. By breaking their silence, and revealing experiences that no child, no human being, should ever have to endure, they give voice to the millions of survivors, and non-survivors (indeed all incest victims do not survive, as Toni Morrison's fictional account of incest demonstrates) whose stories are not told and not heard. If incest is ever to be eradicated, exposure of the crime is imperative. We are grateful for all the women who participated in this project, directly and indirectly, and who were willing to expose themselves in the selfless act of participating in the construction of incest stories.

We extend thoughts of gratitude as well to those women and men whose lived experiences and voiced narratives have inspired and continue to inspire, among them Blackie, Editha, Ma'a, Myrts, Cynthie, Nat, Merle, Lita, Grace, Ros, Lena, Virginia, Gladys, Marlene, Jacqueline, Ginny, Darlene, Susan, Linda, and Little Suzie, as well as Pappy, Newton Egbert, Everton, Lisle, Billy, Bobby, and Bennie.

Introduction

෨෬

O nce upon a time, there was a little girl who dreamed of having a normal family, the kind she saw on television, with a mommy and a daddy, because she had nobody she could call "daddy." She thought she had got her wish the Christmas she was seven when her mommy married a tall, strong man from Sunday school. Six months later, her dream became a nightmare when her new daddy took her into her parents' bedroom, took down the Bible from the dresser, placed her small hand on it, and made her swear that she would never tell what was going to happen. He said it was all because he loved her.

"There were many times when I wondered if the horrible memories I had were fiction—a result of an overactive imagination. Did I imagine the Bible incident? The coming-to while walking to school? And the humiliating orgasm?" (Destiny, in an interview by Hurley, D.L., 2007).

The moment we hear "Once upon a time," we know we are going to be transported to the realm of fantasy. This narrative convention is a signal alerting the listener that what we are about to hear should not be considered as lived reality, that the story that is going to be told has been constructed, that the narrator is not necessarily the author of the story or even a character in it, that the plot is not necessarily focused primarily on the narrator, and that the events related are ordered to be coherent. As George S. Howard asserts in "Culture Tales: A Narrative Approach to Thinking, Cross-cultural Psychology, and Psychotherapy":

> One typically begins a fairy tale with the phrase "Once upon a time." This introduction serves to tip-off the reader as to the genre of the story being offered. Thus, when the author speaks of fairies, dragons, leprechauns, and the like, the listener is not unduly troubled—for imaginary creatures routinely roam the world of fantasy. Lots of strange, fanciful possibilities can be comfortably entertained in a fictitious story. But there are other story forms in which talk of fictitious creatures is forbidden. (187)

In the case with which this book opens, "Once upon a time" introduces, not a fairy tale, but a true story. The events related and the reactions to the events, though related presumably by a third-person narrator, are all the words of the person who lived the experience in real-life. In fact, both the third-person narrator of the first paragraph and the "I" of the second are one and the same individual.

This paradoxical circumstance illustrates one of the central thrusts of this book: the fact that all stories, whether they purport to represent lived or fictional reality, are constructed. Story-telling, the application of a creative impulse for the production and delivery of narratives, is a fundamental feature of existence. It can be asserted authoritatively that everyone almost without exception has told or listened to a story, and has been involved at one time or another, actively or passively, in story-telling. Some narrative creation is intentional, some less so. We all create and construct narratives—the narratives that constitute the reality or perception of, and give meaning to, our lives. In other words, the stories we tell ourselves and the stories that others tell about us often serve as guidelines for the way we live our lives. Some of us create other narratives—fictional narratives, not directly related to our lived experience. But all narratives, fictional or non-fictional, are vehicles by which we come to know ourselves and our societies, and by which we transmit knowledge, hopes, aspirations, ideals, and visions about ourselves and the world in which we live.

Furthermore, it is a semantic truism that the term "story" has multiple and conflicting connotations. It is commonly recognized that while it can signify an account that may be factual, as in a "news story," it can also bear implications of distortion or exaggeration, of imaginative embellishment, of fantasy, of downright untruth. The expression, "constructing incest stories," in the first part of our title, is intended to draw attention to the ambiguities that characterize the process of story-telling and the convergences and differences that exist between non-fictional and fictional stories in the context of incest.

The telling of the story of a real-life experience is dependent on at least two factors: linguistic competence and memory. The importance of these two factors is amplified in the case of experiences that occur at a comparatively young age, where the crucial question is: how does one tell a story when the story itself begins before one has the language for it, before memory or the capacity to retain memory becomes grounded? The incest story is different from other kinds of stories because of the nature of the experience of incest and the peculiar space incest occupies in relation to communication about the experience: the experience is difficult for anyone to relate, and incest is not a fit subject for polite social conversation. In most cases, incest victims who do tell *cannot* usually tell the whole story, because the limitations on their life experience as well as on their vocabulary make the story-telling process too challenging.

Some incest victims are afraid that if they tell they will be accused of telling stories and are convinced they will not be believed. Indeed, it is the common experience of many incest victims as children to be accused of telling stories, of lying. As a result many never tell their story, and many go through adulthood and forget they have an incest story to tell. Therefore many if not most incest stories remain untold. The consequences of this repression of narration are typically severe. In many cases, the untold story ends up devouring incest victims in a variety of horrible ways: it can dismantle entirely their sense of self and reinforce the conviction that they have no worth as a human being. The untold story, moreover, can be the tinder that triggers the conflagration of any number of social and personality disorders, including alcoholism, drug addiction, and prostitution.

For some women who have experienced incest or childhood sexual abuse, there may be a period of time when the memory of the abuse incidents becomes shaded, to the point where even the survivor is unclear whether the incidents were fact or fiction. The disconnect between the horrific experience and the idealized image of what a child's life is supposed to be, as depicted on television or in children's books, often leads the survivor to question whether the experience was real, especially since there is usually no one to witness and validate the experience. Therefore, the question of fact or fiction is central to any discussion of the telling of an incest story. The ambiguity that frequently exists between fact and fiction is of particular importance in relation to the two focal polarities of this book: incest and the process of story-telling or narration.

Let us first attempt to bring some clarity to our use of these terms. It is significant that the word "incest" tends to be used, in the contemporary context, by social science researchers as well as by governmental agencies, as one manifestation of a larger societal problem and is most often included under the umbrella of the more popular term, "childhood (or child) sexual abuse." The "official" definition for child abuse, adopted by the 1974 Child Abuse Prevention and Treatment Act—amended by Congress 1984, includes reference to incest:

(1) the employment, use, persuasion, inducement, enticement, or coercion of any child to engage in, or having a child assist any other person to engage in, any sexually explicit conduct (or any simulation of such conduct) for the purpose of producing any visual depiction of such conduct, or

(2) the rape, molestation, prostitution, or other form of sexual exploitation of children, or incest with children, under circumstances which indicate that the child's health or welfare is harmed or threatened thereby. (Hurley, 2004, 83-4)

The definitions adopted by the most respected researchers make no meaningful distinction between childhood sexual abuse (CSA) and incest. A. Browne & D. Finkelhor (1986) defined incest as "any forced or coerced sexual behavior imposed on a child, and sexual activity between a child and a much older person, whether or not obvious coercion is involved" (66). Nancy D. Vogeltanz et al. (1999) give a variety of definitions for incest, which take into specific consideration the age of the victim and the age differential between victim and perpetrator:

a) any intrafamilial sexual activity before age 18 and that was unwanted or that involved a family member 5 or more years older than the respondent;

b) any extrafamilial sexual activity that occurred before age 18 and was unwanted, or that occurred before age 13 and involved another person 5 or more years older than the respondent...

c) any unwanted extrafamilial activity that occurred before age 14, or any unwanted sexual intercourse occurring at ages 14-17. (582)

Incest or childhood sexual abuse is apparently common among all segments of American society and its importance as a feature of social life is related to its prevalence, which has been estimated by Melissa A. Polusny and Victoria M. Follette (1995) as ranging from fifteen to thirty-three percent in the general female population. These researchers also found that women with histories of CSA did not differ from women without CSA in education, marital status, or ethnicity, and that there were four variables significantly associated with increased risk of CSA: father's drinking, mother's drinking, perception of one's father and mother as rejecting rather than loving, and not living with both biological parents by age sixteen.

As far as story-construction or story-telling is concerned, while a discussion of narrative theory is outside the scope of this book, we would like to examine briefly some of the components and significance of narration, insofar as it relates to the telling of incest stories, and to reflect on what constitutes narrative in this context and what is involved in the process of narration.

Some of the characteristic features of the incest situation—the rejection of the "truth" as told by the victim, the resulting disorientation and instability of the personality of the victim as a telling subject, and the difficulty for the victim to remember and make sense of her experience—are particularly relevant to the activity and significance of story-telling. Incest serves as an excellent lens through which to examine some of the problematics of narration.

Narrative, the exercise of story-telling, involves the application of forms of organization, structure, and control, which provide intelligibility, congruity, and cohesion, and it is this structural dimension that contributes to our (readers' and audience's) acceptance of the verisimilitude of the story. We can indeed accept the assertion made by I.B. Cebik (1986) in "Understanding Narrative Theory" that the only truth relevant to narrative lies in coherence (64).

As we shall see in the chapters that follow, telling an incest story, whether fact or fiction, involves confronting a number of challenges that are characteristic of the art of narration: the identity of, and relationship between, author and narrator(s), the instability of the narrating persona(s), the relative plausibility and stability of the characters, the question of the relative linearity of the story, the sequencing adopted for bringing coherence to the narrative, the outcome of the story, favorable or unfavorable, desirable or undesirable, and the ending that determines its worth within the value system to which we (as readers) subscribe.

According to Cebik, narratives, even fictional narratives, may persuade us to alter the ways in which we perceive and conceive the world around us. Indeed, narrative has an explanatory function. It can express determining conditions and imbue events with meaning or significance. A single narrative can function diversely to educate, edify, inform, correct, revise, update, entertain, inspire actions or attitudes, imbue with value, explain, prove a thesis or establish a theme, reform, revolutionize, teach by example, persuade or convince: for example of the correctness of what has happened or how to view it (73). As a narrative, the incest story (whether fictional or not) can fulfill any and all of these functions.

In this context, there is little difference between lived experience and the experience related in a fictional text. Telling the story requires some construction—an ordering and interpretation of the experience, whether real (lived) or imagined. The experience acquires meaning and makes sense to the extent that a narrative, whether voiced or unvoiced, is constructed about it, and the meaning of the experience is related to the context—social, cultural, and political—in which it is embedded.

The moment, however, we begin to broach the idea of telling tales of incest, we find ourselves confronted by a fundamental contradiction. Childhood sexual abuse, within the context of the dominant social and linguistic systems of North America, is considered a taboo. The subject of incest or of childhood sexual abuse is typically unvoiced and deemed inappropriate for family and other social conversations. Victims of these forms or violence are typically, and within many African diaspora family systems, discouraged from disclosing their experiences either orally or in writing. The real-life narration of such abuse often causes listeners, whether part of the family system or not, to cringe or take refuge in silence.

Originally, the term "taboo" was used within Polynesian societies to refer to a system of prohibitions connected with things considered holy or unclean (Tonga [Polynesia]: *tabu* = holy, unclean). Later the associative field of the term expanded to include any recognized or general prohibition, interdict, restraint, ban, exclusion, or ostracism. In *Incest: A New Perspective* (2002), Mary Hamer points out that naming something as "taboo" implies that it is to be avoided even in discussion: the object of taboo is placed beyond the reach of language (31). Thus, the idea of telling a story about incest presents a veritable linguistic paradox: inserting into language something that is supposed to be beyond the reach of language.

Therefore, this taboo associated with incest should tend to deter not only discussion or narration but even the perpetration of the offence. The prevalence of incest, however, complicates and even contradicts the force of the taboo. Dorothy L. Hurley (1991), in "Women, Alcohol and Incest: An Analytical Review," reports on L. Armstrong's questioning whether childhood sexual abuse in the form of incest is truly a universal taboo. Hurley agrees with Armstrong that the very prevalence of such abuse (a reported one to four million American women having experienced incest) suggests that the incest taboo is not a true deterrent. Hurley asserts that the real taboo may not be incest (the abuse acts and experiences), but talking about it. Since an estimated twenty-two percent of CSA histories are unreported, narrative silence and secrecy seem to be almost inevitable components of childhood sexual abuse.

Telling the incest story is affected by another feature of the incest experience. Telling presupposes a form of agency—the assumption of the role of speaking subject. The assumption of such a role requires some form of power—the exercise of the ability to speak independently, to have a voice. However, an imbalance of power (male/female, adult/child) is a prerequisite condition for the perpetration of incest. Incest is overwhelmingly an abuse of power, conducted in the large majority of cases by males on young girl children. This power imbalance has particular significance in relation to two salient features of social life in the United States: gender relations and race relations. Males in this social context are still perceived as invested with unequal privilege in many areas (physical strength, salaries, certain careers, even the political arena). Moreover, the argument for the existence of a hierarchy that places white males at the top of the social, political, and economic ladder and black females at the bottom is still valid.

The persistence of patriarchy in the privileging of male voices and male perspectives introduces a curious element into the perception and representation of incest. In this context, the notion of incest as an abuse of power tends to be de-emphasized and incest is projected and even justified as an exploration of pleasures that are delicious and unreasonably forbidden, secret and unfamiliar (Hamer, 30). This is the argument that perpetrators of incest and child sexual abuse, predominantly male, seek to disseminate and defend.

Validation of the notion of incest as a form of justifiable sexual pleasure for males requires the suppression of the voices of the (female, child) victims. For this reason, the incest taboo is in effect an injunction to silence. The victim is prohibited from speaking, from disclosure of the offence. When nothing is said, the silence signifies that no opposition is voiced, and so by default the offence becomes permissible and socially sanctioned. Therefore, silence ultimately functions to condone and justify. Since women are the primary victims of the abuse perpetrated most often by men, women are the group who are particularly required to be silent, and the silence and secrecy imposed by the incest taboo are particularly applicable to them. Thus, in the context of gender and race relations in the United States and the place occupied by black women within the prevailing hierarchy of power, the ultimate effect of the incest taboo is the silencing of black women's voices.

The question of voice, because of the experience of people of African heritage in the Americas in the context of European enslavement of Africans and the establishment of plantation societies that placed restrictions on African expressivity, has been for centuries an abiding concern for African-heritage people. The relationship between incest and voice suppression is of particular significance to black women in the United States. Incest, as we have indicated, may be considered as one of the most socially reprehensible forms of the abuse of power and of the violation of a human being imaginable. From the perspective of African-heritage people, incest bears similarities with the form of slavery that occurred in the Atlantic slave trade, in the perpetration of acts of physical and emotional violence on Africans and their descendants and the repression and devaluation for centuries of voices of opposition.

In the documentation and narration of American history, in the context of white domination and patriarchy by which this history is characterized, the voices of women in general, irrespective of their racial or ethnic affiliation, had been for centuries suppressed. Even within white society, women's voices were typically ignored or disregarded, particularly at the level of public discourse. At that level, black female voices for centuries had no currency whatsoever. Impositions placed on the use of indigenous languages, on expressivity through drums, dance, and religious practices, as well as the forced necessity to acquire competency in the dominant European language, while access to books and formal schooling was initially denied and later restricted, paradoxically ensured the value attributed to voice in its many forms in African-heritage people. Only in the 19th century did the black female voice, always mediated by a white authoritative, validating voice, begin to reach the public ear. All the while, however, story-telling, well entrenched in the cultural tradition of griots across many ethnic African societies, survived as a valued and valuable mechanism of survival, resistance, and cultural continuity for black women and men.

The current text took shape in recognition of the significance of voice within the black community and in response to the relationship between incest and story-telling. The present volume arose out of two initially separate projects: on the one hand, Dorothy Hurley's qualitative research into the perceptions of female incest survivors in relation to alcoholism (an initial study that examined the correlation between childhood incest and the development or non-development of alcoholism in women survivors was published in *Alcoholism Treatment Quarterly*, 1991); on the other, E. Anthony Hurley, whose readings of Caribbean and African literature in French (see *Through a Black Veil: Readings of French Caribbean Poetry*, 2000) had convinced him that writing and voice meant something different for African-heritage Blacks in the Americas than for the dominant white community in the European and Euro-American cultural context and who had begun to investigate the problematics of narrating the unnarratable and the construction of narratives particularly by the African-heritage community.

In the course of the research project on the perceptions of incest survivors, Dorothy Hurley interviewed a number of incest survivors. In order to gather meaningful and consistent data on perceptions, she used the protocol of a semi-structured interview administered to a variety of female subjects. When the data were collected, she determined that an effective way of presenting and dramatizing the perceptions of these subjects was to reconstruct the actual words—the responses to specific questions—of the subjects into coherent narratives. Therefore, the recorded interviews developed into a set of well-organized first-person, authentically autobiographical, narratives, designated as "profiles."

For both of us these profiles incited questions about the nature of narrative construction: What was the process by which disjointed utterances—responses to questions—become a narrative? What essential elements constitute the narrative? Who was the "author" of these narratives? What role did the author play? Whose narrative voice was involved in the telling of the story? What role did the narrator play in these narratives? What place did incest play in the narratives? What purpose was served by the constructed narration? This final question was particularly vital, since we recognized that a fundamental aspect of incest was the aura of taboo that surrounds the term. Since incest was to a large extent unmentionable, not to be talked about, and certainly not to be narrated, what could therefore be the function and purpose of incest stories deliberately constructed and voiced or published?

Subsequently, E. Anthony Hurley, in seeking to explore further in a pedagogical context the challenges of narrative theory and construction raised by these "profiles," developed and taught a course at Stony Brook University, entitled "Narrating Abuse in African American Literature," incorporating the incest "profiles" into a comparative examination of real-life and fictional narratives of childhood sexual abuse. Students examined the existing social science research findings on incest/childhood sexual abuse, were introduced to theories and techniques of narrative construction, and read a sample of the factual constructed narratives created from interviews with incest survivors as well as some fictional texts. The factual narratives were used as pedagogical aids to demonstrate some of the technical challenges involved in narrative construction, to serve as a basis for analyzing fictional incest narratives, and to provide a template for the creation by students of their own fictional incest stories. Students were invited to examine and compare the ways in which both the profiles and the fictional incest stories exemplified the theories and techniques of narrative construction. Furthermore, students were required over the course of the semester to construct, after several revisions and rewritings, critiqued at each stage by classmates and by the instructor, a substantial fictional narrative of their own built around the core focus of incest.

This book is an expansion of that research project and that course. The challenge is to produce an unconventional, cross-disciplinary, study that combines social science and literary research methodologies and analyses. Our aim is to present the "truth" about incest, told both from the inside (by survivors) and the outside (by writers of fiction), and at the same time to present analyses of the mechanism of narrative construction, while discussing the challenges involved in constructing an incest story. In so doing, our hope is that this book will validate story-telling for incest survivors, affirm the right of every incest victim to tell her story, and applaud writers who write fictional accounts of incest, thereby telling stories for those who cannot tell them.

The project arises out of a number of considerations: the awareness of the prevalence of incest and childhood sexual abuse; the awareness of the difficulty of actually talking about incest because of the cultural taboo associated with it; and the hope of contributing toward the destruction of the taboo and thereby toward the eradication of the practice of the violation of incest. Such a project raises its own related concerns: What could possibly be the purpose of writing about such a subject? Who would be interested? What good would it do? Two major pitfalls exist: one, the academic, and two, the sensational. We have attempted, therefore, to avoid over-academizing and over-intellectualizing the subject, and at the same time to avoid sensationalizing experiences that carry so much pain.

This book examines the creation of narratives in both fact and fiction, specifically using incest as a focal component because of the overwhelming need for these stories to be told. We examine the narration of childhood sexual abuse in the context of the following questions: How does one talk about something that is not to be talked about? How does one tell a story that is prohibited? How does one narrate the unnarratable? What is involved in such a process? What convergences and differences exist between fictional and non-fictional narratives? What lessons does the story-telling itself hold?

Our contention is that story-telling has immense therapeutic value for survivors, but it also enables the society at large, i.e. people not directly affected by childhood sexual abuse, to cope with, to accept, and to confront an experience which, however common, is usually engulfed in silence. Silence, as we have indicated earlier, is one of the factors that contribute to the continuation of the practice. If incest is not talked about, perhaps we can deny its existence and pretend that it does not really exist—that it is not really occurring. By discussing the stories, and thereby legitimizing story-telling and story construction, we hope that the force of the taboo will be attenuated. We are convinced that whether the story told is fact or fiction, it still serves the important purpose of giving voice to the countless thousands of victims of incest who are in effect voiceless.

We are further convinced that for sexual abuse survivors to read fictional accounts of sexual abuse, in addition to factual testimonies, is cathartic. Fiction is as important as fact in this context. Incest victims may find solace in reading fictional accounts and in fact may not read them as fictional. Non-fictional accounts can be sincere, powerful, moving, and authentic, but their perspective can be limited because of the simplicity and linearity of the narration and the lack of other voices and perspectives. Fiction often provides more detail in relation to contextual description and expressions of reactions and feelings than factual accounts contain. Fictional accounts can be paradoxically more vivid, even rawer, than real-life narratives. They can be constructed without self-consciousness, without the filters used in public or private personal narration. Fiction can provide the illusion of protection, a blindfold, a screening from the judgment of the audience. Moreover, fiction can, and does, complement factual reports. Indeed, what may appear to be fiction or fantasy may often be fact.

In Part I of *Constructing Incest Stories*, titled "Fact," Chapter I presents four real-life accounts of incest (by subjects given the names of Ashley, Gabrielle, Destiny, and Kayla) which were developed from interviews with black women conducted personally by the authors and which have been constructed into first-person stories of the real-life experiences of incest survivors, using their own words. The process of the construction of these "factual" stories serves as a mechanism for examining the dynamics and problematics of narrative construction as manifested in the five fictional works we analyze.

In Part II, titled "Fiction," we present analyses of five fictional texts whose plots are built around incest or childhood sexual abuse incidents: Karen E. Quinones Miller's *I'm Telling* (New York: Simon & Schuster, 2002), Donna Hill's *In My Bedroom* (New York: St. Martin's Press, 2004), Sapphire/ Ramona Lofton's *Push* (New York: Random House, 1996; Vintage, 1997), Alice Walker's *The Color Purple* (New York: Washington Square Press, 1982), and Toni Morrison's *The Bluest Eye* (New York: Penguin, 1970; Plume, 1994). Analyzing these texts, we seek to reflect on the role the incest experience plays in relation to the narrative as a whole, and the questions raised by this representation. We focus specifically on African American women's voices, from the perspective of the injunction to silence imposed by the incest taboo and the overarching ideological context of racism which devalues these women and inhibits communication. The fundamental question we seek to answer is: how (by what specific techniques) does one tell a story that cannot be told, particularly if you are a black woman? This part of our book provides an answer to this question and reflects on the therapeutic, social, and psychological utility of narrative construction in this context.

Both the non-fictional and the fictional stories that we examine confirm that the telling of these stories provides different perspectives on, and interpretations of, a common real-life experience. The process of telling is, in the case of all of the stories, artificial: the stories are all constructed interpretations of reality. However, through the telling of these stories the "truth" about incest emerges. And this truth is applicable to the fictional as well as the non-fictional narratives. As George S. Howard reminds us, "We are in the process of creating value in our lives—of finding the meaning of our lives. A life becomes meaningful when one sees himself or herself as an actor within the context of a story" (196). Our hope is that the narratives that follow and the framing narrative of our analysis and interpretation will contribute to a new narrative of unsilenced voices.

PART I

FACT

Chapter One

IN THEIR OWN WORDS

ঌ•ঌ

Adult women participating in an incest survivors' support group that was facilitated by a clinical social worker were given the therapeutic task of writing their stories. Many of the survivors had never told their stories outside the context of therapy, except for those who had disclosed their abuse to family members, most often their mothers, and in many cases they had not been believed. The process of writing made their stories real for these women who were then encouraged to disclose the "truth" of their experiences in a semi-public forum by reading their written narratives out loud in their group. Thus, writing, reading, and listening to survivor narratives were a means of validating their experiences and moving these experiences out of the realm of fiction or untruths and into reality. These women produced the original versions of some of the incest stories that were later retold in interviews.

The women all sat in a circle and listened intently, almost reverently, when a survivor read. Many times the reader had difficulty completing the reading because the very act of telling the story resulted in her re-experiencing the pain of the abuse. The circle, however, was always a safe place in which to share. Through the personal relationship developed with some of the survivors and the cooperation of the group clinical social worker, we were able to obtain our sample of the incest survivors, conduct interviews, and later construct narratives using their own words.

During the process of conducting the interviews, all the survivors made it clear that they wanted to tell their stories, and they were even interested in their stories being told on a larger scale, i.e., to a wider audience. Several of them encouraged us to produce a book containing their stories. This desire to be heard by others points to a practical function of fictional narratives. Fictional incest narratives can serve to give voice to countless incest victims and incest survivors who never make it to therapeutic communities, and who never have an opportunity to tell their incest story.

This function of narratives explains the relationship of the different agents that construct incest stories. Researchers of incest/childhood sexual abuse (CSA), clinicians, and writers of fiction converge in the different incest stories they construct in that these varied stories all give form, authentication, and voice to the voiceless in different but related ways. Toni Morrison reveals in her afterword to the *Bluest Eye* that the impetus for her constructing the incest tale in her novel was the real-life story of a childhood friend. Susan Forward, a social science researcher and co-author (with Craig Buck) of the landmark study, *Betrayal of Innocence: Incest and Its Devastation*, discloses her own experience with childhood sexual abuse in the introduction of this text. Thus, fiction and non-fiction, novelist and scientific researcher converge in validating the experiences and privileging the voices of incest survivors.

The real-life stories of four African American incest survivors, identified by the fictitious names of Ashley, Gabrielle, Destiny, and Kayla, follow in this chapter. To preserve the survivors' anonymity, we have intentionally omitted identifying information. We constructed the stories by conducting 90-120 minute interviews with the survivors based on a semi-structured protocol of questions, transcribing their interviews verbatim, and then organizing their words to create first-person narratives. The interview responses could not by any stretch of the imagination be considered as narratives. We did not ask the interview subjects to develop coherent stories, and neither the interviewer nor the interview subjects intended at the outset to create narratives.

The procedure used to develop these stories raises some questions of relevance to theories and techniques of narration. Who is the author of the narrative? Is it the survivor, the researcher, or both? In what significant ways are these real-life stories different from or similar to fictional narratives? These questions are not addressed directly in this chapter. However, the analyses of fictional stories in succeeding chapters will shed light on these matters. These accounts appear as coherent first-person narratives, as genuine real-life incest stories, in which the voices and words of the incest survivors are faithfully reproduced.

These stories present an interesting insight into narration, raising questions about the personas of author and narrator and about narrative voice and perspective. The "voice" represented in the actual words used is the voice in each case of the incest survivor, but she did not choose the interview questions; nor did she participate in the construction of the story that is reproduced here. We employed a single model (questionnaire and linear organization) for the construction of the stories and therefore function as co-narrators and even "authors" or "co-authors." Our presence and voice are indicated by the punctuation, by the use of brackets and parentheses, and by suspension points that indicate omission of words used by the survivor. Therefore, while the content of each story reproduces the voice of the survivor, the responsibility for the questions and for the form of the stories as they appear lies with us.

ASHLEY'S STORY

I had an alcoholic father and a real Christian goody two-shoes mother. I was the oldest [child]. I had two sisters and one brother. They were okay, they were bright or whatever, but I was bad. I was always getting in trouble and getting my butt beat all the time. I loved stirring up things. That was my way of getting to them. I just didn't like nobody. I hated life. I liked [one of] my sister[s]... the one next to me, I always loved her. But the rest of them, I could[n't] care [less] whether they came or left.

My mother worked, she always worked. I sent the kids off to school and cleaned the house.

There was always tension in my household. It was like my mother was always afraid of something. We had to be real quiet because she would always talk about what he [my father] didn't like. She had a real fear of him. I could never understand that. I was wondering why they really stayed together. They didn't really care about one another. They seemed like they were unhappy, they didn't relate to one another. He was in one world and she was in another. He ran the streets a lot and she stayed home. She made him a god. Anything he said, she believed it.

I didn't feel close to my mother or my father. My mother was a little bit prejudiced. My hair wasn't curly like the rest of them and I was too dark. I wasn't smart like they [sisters and brother] were. [My mother] would always compare. I didn't like that about her since I can remember living on the planet. [Mother] didn't touch. She would do things for you but she wasn't into touching. People have good points. My mother made everybody special, she was a giver. She loved giving of herself and she loved her kids. She would spoil me, I was rotten. All [I had to] do was get sick and cry and she would give me my way. She irritated me being so good. She would do everything his way.

[My father] was one of those strict, stern fathers; he had us like soldiers. It was like being in the army. He worked real hard. He taught us a lot, he taught us how to cook. He taught us things my mother should have taught us, how to cook and clean and how to be ladies. I guess he ... worried to death about his three daughters. He was always like an authority [figure]. Like a school or something. You go to school and you may like your teacher, but you know it's a distance. You can't get too close.

The first time he [my father] attempted [incest] I was seven. I didn't know nothing about sex, but I had a feeling about things. He was home drunk one night and told my mom, "Have her put a dress on." It was late at night. He was taking me to this dark place. I got fearful. He told me to sit on his lap. I left him and ran all the way home and told my mother. He came home with his lies. She took it.

After that, I was nine years old. He would send all the kids off to school. That's when it happened. That day, he told me to stay home. He gave the kids money. They went off to school. I didn't suspect nothing, until after the kids left. I started feeling something was wrong. He raped me and beat me up real bad. Brutalized me real bad. I remember just sitting. I couldn't wait to just get out of there or till my mother came home. I just remember all this fear in me. I remember her [mother] coming home. She just started crying. The cops came. They took me around looking for him. They finally found him. They put him in jail. That's when I really started hating her [my mother] because she believed . . . they go to jail and they come back changed. He [my father] came home with this bible and that's when I really got bad. I said, "What! You believe in him? You let him come back to the house!" [My mother] told me to lie and say that I didn't know what happened when I went to court. The judge threw the case out. He knew they brainwashed me a lot, but what could he do.

[My father] got out of jail and that's when the fighting started between us. If I hadn't fought him, I guess he would have raped me again. By then, I was thirteen and I just made up my mind that I wasn't taking any more crap.

[During adolescence] I was a bitch. My mother used to cry and she used to say [it was] because of like I was. At a young age, I went through a stage in my life that older ladies went into. I would use men. I wouldn't give them nothing but I would sure take money. I mean, from thirteen, I went to old head places. I didn't deal with no children. I grew up too fast. Then, I just changed it around . . . after I almost got raped. I was around fifteen. I started going to church after that. I thought if God could get me out of this one, I'll promise I'll be good and won't disobey my mother. I guess I became a teenager after that.

I really didn't remember [the rape]. It's like I blacked it out until I was around seventeen [when] this boyfriend asked me about it. It brought it back to my memory and I went crazy then. After that I remembered again. It was really painful for me to remember. It made me feel real freaky, like there was something wrong with me.

I grew up real fast. By the time I was twelve I had a body. Everybody was after me. I felt like it was a curse. They would say how nice looking I was and how attractive I was, but I never believed it. I felt like "Miss Dirty." I never felt pretty like some people. My mom put little baby dresses on [me], but they didn't cover it up. Even the ladies would tell me how pretty [I was]. I hated it though, because I thought that [it] would make people attracted to me, especially men. That's how I got into dressing the way I dress. I don't like sexy things.

That experience [incest] and the way my mother was, like a slave instead of a wife, made me kind of hard on men. I'm not waiting on no man hand and foot. It seems like I go into some kind of insanity and I could kill if somebody approached me like that. Since I got raped I just lost faith in people. I didn't trust my parents. I hated living, my life sucked, I hated getting up. I just existed.

I wasn't active [sexually] until my first husband, when I was nineteen. I didn't know nothing about sex because I would black it out. I didn't want to read no sex books. [So] I never realized he [my husband] was a harsh lover. He was sick. He wasn't normal, he was oversexed; he wanted to make love all the time and he really didn't care about me. I was his personal prostitute or something that you pick up. If he said he wanted to make love to me, I'd say okay, if I felt like it or not. I thought that whatever they say you're not supposed to say no. [Eventually] we broke up. After we broke up, I wanted to be normal like other people. I was determined, well, if anything is wrong with me, I damn sure want to find out. What better way to find out than to go make love to people. I went through times when I was a whore but that didn't last long. [Alcohol and drugs] gave me the courage. It would cut off thoughts like, "Am I really a whore?" I really wanted to know. So then I said [to myself], "Well, damn it, we want to find out, we want to see if you're a whore or not. We was going to do whatever comes to our head and see if we like it." And that's what I did. I was a guinea pig and I knew it. I used me as a guinea pig. I did it for a while and I found out that I was just making people have fun and it wasn't making me no fun. I was getting nothing out of it. I was a great actor but I didn't get nothing out of it. They didn't satisfy me.

I hated drinkers. To me people who drank acted crazy. And I tried to be one, late [at] twenty-five. [Before] I was always chasing God. I wanted to seek this higher power because I wanted peace. I always knew I was unhappy. I tried suicide more than once, in all different ways. That was before I even started drinking. I was real shy and at first [alcohol] made me feel witty. I could blend in. [It] took the fear away and I could dance and socialize. I got into alcohol and drugs. [Later, alcohol and drugs] made me a recluse. I didn't mind being alone. I would say that I didn't need people, but at first it made me feel the opposite. I was happy, I could talk and wasn't afraid of going out. I would go everywhere by myself.

I went [to therapy] for my oldest son. He had burnt my house down and I just wanted to find help for him. I knew I didn't really want it, because I didn't want them digging into me. But, I said, "Well, if it will help him, I'll let them dig into me." [In therapy], I lied about my drinking, [but] I didn't lie about [incest].

I never had a lot of friends in my life. It seemed like God always put one or two people in my life. Somebody always liked me a lot. I met this guy. I moved in his house. I was horrible, I would fight the man, accuse him of all kinds of crazy things, but he was still loving to me. I was getting paranoid. I was having the shakes. I had to get up in the morning and take a drink because my hands were shaking. [He said], "There's supposed to be an alcohol program for you. You want me to take you?" . . . In my heart I knew that I needed help. So I found the [AA] program. I was sober for the first time for three years. I found an excuse to drink again.

When I first started recovering, [the incest] came to the surface. I didn't talk about it to nobody. When I came [back] in the program, I talked about it. The more I talked about it, the more it came out until the point where I felt comfortable. I feel like I am better. It's still a problem. I don't like to watch it on TV. But it don't hurt me anymore and I don't feel like a freak anymore. I don't feel like all men are dogs.

I'm normal today. I can enjoy sex with the right person. I really don't want a relationship. I don't want anybody living with me. I got into relationships with married men because they got a wife to go home to. I always get some kind of man [where] I end up being mommy. I don't want that responsibility today. I don't want anybody to depend on me today.

I'm glad for everything that happened to me because I wouldn't be getting the peace of mind I'm getting today. What happened to me [made] me say, "I need help." I didn't want to trust anyone, but it brought me to say I need help and I got to trust people. It made me different and I'm glad for everything.

GABRIELLE'S STORY

Me, my brother, my stepfather (my brother's father) and my mother moved up here from down South. We lived in a very poor part of town. My stepfather did odd jobs and my mother was a houseworker.

I was a scary person and had a lot of violence in my family. There were weekends [when] my mother and my stepfather would fight all the time. My stepfather, he beat her [my mother] every weekend. I wanted to protect her but I couldn't. When they started to fight, I would lose my voice. I would just stand there, just freeze or just pee myself.

I was a sick pup. I didn't like myself, I hated myself. I didn't think I was worth being on this earth. [My mother] hated me. From the very beginning she would always say, "I'll be glad when you kids get the fuck out of my face." She told me I was ugly and I was her problem because I couldn't get my head together. I was always nervous. I would tell her that I was scared of daddy. She said, "You don't know what you is talking about, that's not true." I was always wrong, I wasn't shit.

I loved school. The teachers were nice, they were more understanding. I looked forward to the stars they put on my paper. I was good in school. The kids beat me up a lot because I was country, I dressed country.

My stepfather made it quite clear that I wasn't his child and that he didn't like me. I was scared to death of him. I was about three or four [when my mother] took my brother with her to a funeral and left me with him. He put me on the bed and slapped me around. He would tell me, "Come here." I would come to him and he would say, "You're no fucking good, you ain't my baby." He made me put my mouth on his penis. He'd say, "Don't bite it, just suck it."

[When I was seven, I got a new stepfather]. He was the best, but he was real brutal to my mother. The first stepfather she [mother] stabbed real bad with an ice pick. This one protected me. I felt protected by him because he would always get her to stop slapping me around, stop cursing me out. She took that as him screwing me. She burned him up and split. I drank some Clorox and they took me to St. _____ [hospital and] pumped my stomach out. I went home and got reprimanded about it.

[When I was twelve or thirteen] my uncle tried [to have sex with me]. I was watching TV on the floor and he came in, jumped on top of me, started rubbing against me. [I] told my mother. She told me I was a liar. [After that] it was just no sense in telling her and this continued all the time.

[During adolescence I] did a lot of running away from home. I got caught up with God. I found refuge in God, in the church. I started witnessing on the corners. I wanted to be a minister. [My mother] didn't like the church I was getting caught up in, so I started to run away more and more often. I called child abuse on her several times, but at that time back then, it didn't mean nothing. I showed them the welts on my back. She [mother] would tell them, "She's crazy. The girl's crazy, she acts out in school, she wants attention." So they let me alone. [I told the school counselor] about the incest and stuff. She tried to talk to my mom. She [the counselor] was one of the positive things that made me grow up. She said, "Finish school no matter what." Anyway, my mother cursed her out and said, "All she needs is a good ass whipping."

[I started drinking] at seventeen. [My mother and first stepfather] were both heavy drinkers. At first it [alcohol] made me feel grown, it made me feel like a lady. I could dance and was witty. [I] could talk to older men. It made me feel perfect, it made me feel nice, uninhibited, do all kinds of crazy things.

I hated men. I hate them today and I know it, but I like them too. I like being with them, I like the sharing, hugging and the kissing. I love all that, but I don't believe them. I don't believe that they really love me. I don't believe nothing.

I never think that a relationship could go for a long period of time. It's hard for me to believe that I could marry somebody and we would be together for the rest of our lives.

I married an older man when I was nineteen. He was like my mother. He was aggressive but I had good sex with him. But we couldn't get along. He told me to go get help [for my drinking] when he met me. [I went but I didn't stop drinking]. He was caught up in heroin [and] he died. After he died, I refused to accept the fact that he was dead. I lived in this little [fantasy] world that he would come back. His best friend came around about two months later to get me out of this thing. I thought he was a friend, I really did. I was dumb. He slapped the shit out of me, punched me in my face, got me on the floor, took my ring off, my wedding band, stuck his penis in my mouth, and that broke my heart because I [had] trusted him. That was the turning point. I just started drinking more and more and more, didn't trust nobody, fucked around with everybody. The first time I sought therapy was '75. I got sober in '77. I went to therapy [because] I didn't want to kill myself no more. I didn't want to [attempt] any more suicides. I was scared that I was going to hurt my son. I didn't want him to be abused like me. I started hating him for no reason.

I lied [about drinking]. I would get drunk all night. When I would get ready to go see [the therapist], I would go throw up in the bathroom a couple of hours before I'd go see him. He'd tell me I was a very successful black woman, that I really didn't have no problems, that I'd overcome a lot because I had a good field [career] and I had a couple of college degrees under my belt.

I still cry, I still have nightmares, bloody nightmares. The first couple of years of my recovery they were like every week. Now they're not as often. The booze makes you feel like you're a nobody. Even now in my sexual relationships I'm scared, like the aggressive guy, he wants to please me, I fight him off. I don't think that I should have complete pleasure. The guys that I get along with, the ones that last, that hang around with me long enough, were the ones that had a passive personality. I was the aggressive person in sexual matters. Then, when the guys that are aggressive come after me, I go [in] the opposite direction.

I don't trust people, I don't trust a living ass, but I put myself out there because the program says, "Put yourself out there." I want to trust somebody, but my recovery has been painful when it came to some people that I trusted things with, like my incest and my sexual promiscuity. They have used that against me in their attitude and how they treat me now. I screwed like I was changing drawers when I was drinking. I didn't give a damn, I just screwed anybody I could. Now [it's] 100% changed. [I was] looking for love, looking for that somebody to love. I wanted a daddy, I wanted to be protected.

The first time I [had sex I] was so disappointed. It wasn't nothing. I was angry because I thought I was a virgin. I expected all this pain and blood. I wasn't a virgin. I was broken before, and I didn't know who broke me. All I could think of was the first [stepfather]. He did it.

I could really say that my sex life [while] drinking was unsatisfying. It was mechanical. [Sober], I stopped having so many guys. Since I've been recovering, I've had nine or ten different men. I thought I didn't deserve to have [orgasms] and I still have those feelings now.

I feel vulnerable, especially at work. I feel ... the feminine side of me. If I could have anything in this world, I would like to have total self-confidence. That's the only thing I want. And if I should stop school, if I should stop working, just stop whatever these achievements that I put on myself to prove that I am somebody, just to stop that and just say, "Gabrielle, you're okay today." That's all I want.

DESTINY'S STORY

I was born into sort of a crazy family, on my mother's sixteenth birthday. My father is actually married to my grandmother. My mother told me the way I got to be born: he [mother's stepfather] forced her to have sex with him.

I lived in a house [with] my grandmother, my mother, her sisters, brothers, my father [mother's stepfather], [and] a lot of kids—my cousins—I called them all my cousins.

Somewhere along the line, I found out all those cousins I thought were my cousins were my half sisters and brothers. My father had twenty-two children. Eleven of the children, he had between my mother, her sisters, and my grandmother. It's a bizarre story.

You could say I was pretty happy until I was seven. There were a lot of kids for me to play with. People liked me. I spent a lot of time with my mother. I adored my mother.

[When I was seven] my life changed overnight. My mother told me we were going to have a place of our own [and] a family, the kind of family where there was a mother and father and kids. I had just begun to feel that I was different because I didn't have that. When we moved my mother went to work. Daddy [stepfather] and my mother took the younger kids to my grandmother's. I had to go to school by myself [and] come home [by myself]. The house would be dark and I was afraid.

[Before that time] I lived the life of a child. I didn't have to do housework and I didn't have to take care of any kids because there were always grownups around and I was always being taken care of by somebody. I was always played with, had a lot of attention [and] affection.

My stepfather changed his work shift. He was home when I would come home at lunchtime. One day, he called me into my mother's and his bedroom. I can't remember the details. He had me put my hand on the bible [and] swear that I wouldn't tell anybody. He told me if I ever told her [my mother] that he would leave her. It would be my fault. I loved my mother more than anything in the whole wide world. I couldn't take the responsibility of her losing something that I thought she really wanted. I felt protective. I felt responsible. At the same time it was bad. My mother [had] raised me to be a good girl. Good girls didn't do those kinds of things. I knew good girls were virgins when they got married ... wore white dresses.

After that day, I knew couldn't have any of that any more. It was like no matter what happened after that, it was losing something that I could never have. No matter what, there was no changing it. I didn't have a lot of memory of the years that followed. I don't know how many times I had sex with my stepfather.

Because of the incest I felt inferior. I no longer felt like a child. I wasn't unhappy all the time. I lived in two worlds. I just pretended it wasn't happening. I blocked a lot of it. I was very lonely for a long time.

I used to hope [that] somehow my mother was going to find out and save me. I couldn't save myself. I was very angry years later because I thought my mother should have saved me. She should have known. She should have figured it out. I felt so dirty, just like scum.

I continued to do well in school ... get decent grades. They were never good enough for me. It seemed like I could never be what I wanted to be, like the best or anything.

When I was thirteen, out of my fear of being pregnant, I made the decision to tell my mother. I told her. She went to my stepfather, [came back,] looked me straight in the eyes, and said, "He says it isn't true." Something inside of me froze solid. I just felt numb. I think I felt shock.

At first I remember deciding to kill myself. I got sleeping pills [and] took them. Nothing happened. I got angry. I somehow felt it was me against the world. I just wasn't going to let him win. I wanted to be somebody.

After the incest stopped, things seemed to fall apart. When the incest was still going on, I took care of the house, I took care of the kids. After I told, I stopped babysitting, I stopped cleaning. There were roaches. The furniture fell apart. My stepfather was drinking. You never knew if he was going to come home, pull out a gun, or fight with my mother. [During adolescence] I made a life for myself outside the house. I had friends. I went to parties. I got a boyfriend.

I was very envious of middle class kids. [I] felt that I didn't fit in. I would hang out with the group that didn't fit in either. I started getting into trouble. I started hookeying school. I started stealing things for attention. I cut classes. I'd get suspended.

The first time I remember drinking, I was about fifteen. I got high and felt wonderful. I think my use of alcohol and the incest are connected. The incest left me feeling frightened, untrustful, self-conscious, inferior, unattractive, unsure of myself, inadequate, and at the same time prideful and angry. Alcohol was a way of medicating those feelings. Alcohol worked for me. My use of alcohol, at one point, was an attribute. I impressed people with it. It was a way of fitting in, being a part of. My boyfriend was impressed by the way I drank. This was the same man I married.

I sort of expected my life to be different from other people. I thought I was lucky that I didn't have a nervous breakdown or that I wasn't a criminal or wasn't on drugs. I used to feel guilty because my life seemed so good compared to my brothers and sisters.

I got married. I felt really lucky to have him [my husband]. I really felt like damaged goods. I had this fear [that] if he wasn't in my life there wouldn't be anybody else. I felt like I didn't know how to make it with guys. He would say a lot of negative things to me on a regular basis. We separated more than once. The third time, I left him.

I had been friends with a woman who was a mothering type. I knew she was gay. One day I propositioned her. I knew I wasn't gay, but she was so warm, loving, nurturing, and taking care of. I wanted that. I could give of myself sexually in order to get it back. It was a bargain I made in my mind. It solved the problem with me being afraid I was inadequate with men. I didn't have to face that failure by being involved with a woman.

I initially decided to go to therapy because I looked at the relationships in my life and knew that something was wrong. I especially got depressed around love relationship issues. I drank [and] used sex for depression. Relationships were the catalyst in me going to therapy and also for me eventually dealing with my alcoholism.

I was getting ready to get discharged from therapy. My therapist knew nothing about alcoholism. I was under the impression that [if] I ever worked through my incest issues I would stop abusing alcohol, stop drinking too much at certain times, like the time I crashed my car.

It [all] went back to what I originally went to therapy for. I would feel that I was okay if I was capable of having a healthy relationship with a man. I met Prince Charming. I gave a dinner party one night in his honor. We ended up having a vicious argument. It was a blackout [for me]. The relationship ended. I felt guilty, I felt responsible. I went into a depression.

[The night of] my last drink, I had an out-of-the-body experience. I knew I didn't have any control anymore. I decided I would kill myself. I just had too much pride for everybody to find out I was a real loser. I was worse off than any of them, meaning my family. The next morning I called AA.

One of the ways [incest] affected me is … I don't think I ever learned the difference between love and sex. If sex was my choice, I felt love. If sex wasn't my choice, if it wasn't initiated or manipulated by me, then I would feel used. Until I got sober I couldn't have orgasms unless I had alcohol and marijuana. Even sober I have difficulty relaxing for sex. Even though I'm in a very healthy, very happy relationship, sex continues to be a difficult area.

I don't think there is full recovery when it comes to incest, [but] I think I've recovered tremendously. It's not a secret. I'm no longer ashamed of the incest. It surprises me that there is still pain. I still hurt, but there is no longer shame. I no longer feel guilty, I no longer feel responsible, I no longer feel angry.

I believe today that a healthy relationship is possible for me. It is difficult. Some of the scars from my past come into it from time to time. I am married to a very loving, understanding man.

The way I feel about myself is very different. I'm still pretty hard on myself but deep down there is a growing feeling of me being more than okay. There are times when I feel almost like the princess I did before the incest.

KAYLA'S STORY

I don't remember a whole lot of my childhood. I think I was an invisible child. I was good and I was quiet. I tried to be an invisible person.

I was the oldest girl of six children. I had a tremendous amount of responsibility. I took on a lot of tasks. My way of protecting myself was to be busy and to be with people. I remember trying to be a perfect kid, get all A's, help around the house. I would do anything for praise. I was kind of used as a child and since I was such a nice kid, I did a lot. I remember my mother having her last child. I was twelve years old. I took off from school for five days to take care of my family. It never occurred to me how much I took care of my mother. I don't remember being taken care of. If someone tried to take care of me, I tried to be a perfect little person for them. There was so much of my energy put into it that I hardly felt theirs.

[My family] was an organized family. There was this sense of family and love. When it wasn't normal it was a cold family. I would do anything to make it normal.

My father was a striver and worked hard. My mother, I remember wanting her, for years, years and years, to just love me and not really getting much from her.

I think I was abused up until age five. My grandfather lived with us [and] my grandfather died when I was eight. I believe it was an oral genital contact. I believe I told my parents. I believe they lied to me and said it would be okay. The flashbacks to me were like a movie where I would see every fourth frame. I would be missing pieces of it.

The most difficult thing for me to do was tell my parents. Their responses validated what I needed validated even though there was no kind of gathering around or what I wanted in terms of emotional support. But the validation of the incest was there because of the strange things they said about my grandfather.

When I was thirteen or fourteen, I was afraid of the sexuality that was coming up. I had difficult peer relationships. I wanted my peers to love me. I didn't like the kind of petty, catty stuff that goes on with girls. I had this group of girlfriends that I was very close with. They said that I had sexual relations and I hadn't. I felt like they turned on me and I never trusted after that.

I went to college. I dropped out after the first year. Then I got pregnant with my daughter and then I got married. [Soon after] I started to go back [to college]. I always felt not good enough. I started taking psych courses. [I thought], well if I wasn't going to have intimate relationships with people, at least I would understand why. So I went to undergraduate school for thirteen years.

My husband was a perfect complement to me. [He] was very afraid of intimate relationships, was also frightened of losing me, and at the same time didn't treat me very well. We weren't close emotionally. I ended up going to graduate school and having an affair. I believe [my husband] wanted a divorce for a long time and didn't have the nerve to get it. I did all the work for him. I had the affair and that was the break up of my marriage.

I went to therapy around that break-up and [to find out] why I was having an affair. I was married for fifteen years and never had an affair, never thought I'd have an affair, and then I turn around and have an affair.

I'd been in therapy for years on and off. I didn't remember the incest until I was thirty-seven. I was quitting therapy and my therapist said: "You really have to deal with the sexual abuse issue with your grandfather." And I had never heard me say it. I quit [therapy] and I called her three days later: "I don't think I should quit." I went back into therapy.

I started to remember [the incest] in flashbacks. I was very, very frightened that I would remember more and more and more. I had a flashback where I was disassociated from the incident; it was like I was looking down from the ceiling into the bed and saw myself struggling. I thought I was going crazy.

When I found out about the incest, it was like my whole life fit together. [However], it bothers me that when I thought I had control over myself, it [incest] affected who I married, the job I did, how I raised my children. It had such a widespread effect. [The incest] affected my whole life. I think it affected the way I relate to people, the way I feel during sex: I feel in control, I feel the power, I don't feel love, I don't feel orgasm.

By the time I was sixteen I had had sexual intercourse and considered myself very, very good in bed in the sense that I could use my sexuality to get a relationship established. I used sex to get close and then I'd back up. I used sex to connect. I feel like [sex] is the answer to any emotion, if you are mad, sad or glad, "let's go to bed." I just can't hang in there with deep sadness. I found it devastating.

I think what broke up my marriage was that my husband went through a midlife crisis and was having sexual problems. I took that real personally, as if that was my fault.

My sexual history feels strange to me because it's so easy for me to get somebody in bed, but I don't go to bed with a lot of people and that's the control in me. [In] sexual relationships I would say that I am the leader, I am the controller of the relationship. I think [the incest] affected my ability to have an orgasm. I think I've had orgasms, but not that many considering how much I like sex. I think [it's] kind of the curse of control. I think that I need to control [the sexual] act, I need to stay in control, and when I have an orgasm I feel like I'm out of control...

I also have a lot of masochistic tendencies. I could experience orgasms if I read sado/mascochistic stuff [first], which I find really weird.

I tend to have long-lasting relationships. Even since I've been divorced I've had a series of really long [term] relationships. I'm attracted to very powerful, ambitious, workaholic men [and] I pick emotionally limited men as partners.

I dated people that don't drink at all or they are alcoholic. There doesn't seem to be a medium. I don't drink a lot, I never liked drinking. I hate the feeling when I'm out of control. I can't stand not being in control. I would never dull my senses; that would be the last thing in the world I would want to happen to me. No one in my family is an alcoholic that I know of. [However], my mother or my sister may end up alcoholic. They both happened to be under a lot of stress [and] they were drinking every night together, a lot. I would consider it alcoholic drinking.

I don't know if I will ever recover from [incest]. I'm still working on it. As I've learned to live with myself, probably the hardest thing I ever had to do was to be by myself for a period of time because I didn't feel very protected. [Today] I don't have to have someone live with me. [I don't] have this dying urge to get married again [or an] incredible need for a man in my life that I used to. I think I'm in search of a healthier relationship.

Recovery for me is getting my life to be some kind of a normal pace. I usually have to have a lot of activity. I usually have so many things going on that I'm always at stress level. I think the reason that I have an overactive schedule is that it became a life habit. When I was quiet I would have flashbacks. Every time I turn around, the incest creeps into my life again. It interferes with something that I do that I think is healthy and I really resent that.

PART II

FICTION

Chapter Two

POPULARIZING THE UNSPEAKABLE: *I'M TELLING*

❧❧❧

Karen E. Quinones Miller's *I'm Telling* adapts the incest story to the popular fiction market. The title is provocative in many ways. It clearly announces an intention to provide a personal narrative and in so doing it alludes to an issue that is central to the generation of interest and suspense in many fictional narratives: a secret to be revealed. This suggestion of a threat of public disclosure appeals to the attraction to gossip which is such an important part of popular cultural practice in the United States and elsewhere. In this way, the title may generate interest related to the fascination with scandal which the content of the narrative promises to justify. Since silence serves as an effective means of perpetuating the incest system, the title hints at a decision to break this taboo. In this way, the title positions the narrative on a moral high ground that reinforces the mechanism for dismantling the system that facilitates the perpetuation of incest, even though, in relation to the plot of the novel, telling makes no difference whatsoever.

The reality of incest is difficult to represent narratively in ways that may be considered as positive. An incest story cannot easily be transformed into "light" reading. Given the indisputable fact that incest may accurately be considered as not only physically and emotionally horrible, morally reprehensible, disgusting, vile, and abhorrent, but literally and socially unspeakable, how can incest be narrated in a way to make an account of it palatable and even enjoyable to readers of popular fiction? One way of achieving this goal would be to displace the horrific aspects of the incest experience as the primary center of interest in relation to plot and use incest as a conduit for stimulating interest in other plot elements that are less objectionable and more acceptable. This is the narrative strategy that Miller adopts in her novel. While the incest motif is introduced early, on the one hand Miller's narrator relates the incest acts in a way calculated to generate in readers not so much revulsion as prurient interest and, on the other, the narrative provides alternative focuses of plot interest which mitigate the negativity of the incest experience. In this story, the incest experience, though undoubtedly horrible, is related in such a way that it may be viewed as an essentially sexual activity, the deviant nature of which may arouse salacious interest rather than disgust or abhorrence. The narrative center of interest is further displaced by not focusing on incest itself, and by not making Hope, the incest victim, the protagonist, but rather on privileging the perspective, the dilemma, and the activities of Faith, her twin sister, the witness to, and primary narrator of, the incest.

Faith frames the story and provides its narrative core. The main plot threads are woven around her dilemma in relation to disclosure and the more mundane challenges of her life— her attempt to maintain and develop a healthy relationship with a man in the face of the complex links of responsibility that bind her to an emotionally damaged twin sister and an even more twisted mother.

This displacement of interest affects the very structure of the novel, which is divided into a prologue, followed by seventeen numbered chapters. There is no titled epilogue, although the final chapter functions as one, since it relates incidents that occur more than six months after those of Chapter 16. The novel opens with a first-person Prologue in which Faith recounts her experience of witnessing, at around age eleven, an incest incident perpetrated by her stepfather on her twin sister, Hope: "My stepfather's face in between my twin sister's legs" (1). It ends in almost fairy-tale fashion with a surprise wedding between Faith and Henry, the first and only love of her life.

This structure, which highlights Faith's multiple activities and concerns, is supported by the strategy of presenting variations in narrative perspective. While, for instance, the title directly announces a first-person narrative, the narrative as a whole is not a first-person narrative. First-person narration occurs directly only in the prologue (pages 1-5). There is therefore a contradiction or ambiguity in narrative perspective in relation to the title and prologue on one hand, and the remainder of the narrative.

A similar ambiguity in narration occurs in Chapter 2 (42-46), in a section in italics which is supposed to represent a flashback relating to a scene that took place several years before the period covered in the diegetic present of the novel. This segment is explained as a dream or nightmare experienced by Faith. But the very clarity of the details makes such an interpretation difficult to accept. More troubling from a narrative standpoint, even though the narration in this section is conducted ostensibly in the third person, and refers to Faith in the third person, the narrator employs the term "Mommy" to refer to Faith's mother. Whether this ambiguity is deliberate or merely a narrative or copy-editorial slippage remains unclear. The use of this personal term, however, invites the interpretation that the third-person narrator is a cloak for Faith herself.

What is the effect or function of this misdirection in the story-telling strategy? The idea, signaled in the title, of a personal testimony, with its characteristics of "authenticity" in relation to the sharing of experience and the establishment of a privileged relationship and communication with the reader, persists even when the novel proper adopts the more impersonal third-person narrative perspective. Thus, in contrast to the objectivity often associated with third-person narration, the voice, attitudes, and opinions of Faith, the original first-person narrator, are privileged throughout.

The testimonial force of first-person narration, with its implicit presumption of authenticity and even veracity, is employed to relate Hope's incest experience. The incest perpetrated on Hope is presented through two first-person narrative perspectives: first by Faith's account in the Prologue as an observer, and later by Hope herself as, in her mind, an instigator rather than a victim (167). The difference in narrative perspective correlates with the difference in character and attitude between the twin sisters and is used as a technical strategy to highlight the difference between victim and non-victim.

The main characters in this novel tend to be crudely drawn, almost caricatures. Faith is the successful twin, contrasted with her younger sister, Hope, whose life is in a shambles. Faith's love interest, Henry, is presented as an idealized stereotype of young African American manhood, who has a past of black ghetto life, of selling drugs to support his family and his education, as well as Nation of Islam (Black Muslim) conditioning, and who has become a well educated and highly successful investment banker and a romanticized lover who enjoys engaging in erotic role play. The stepfather is similarly stereotypical as an incest perpetrator, indulging in bouts of sexual, physical, and verbal abuse indiscriminately to women and young girls. The mother, Irene, is self-centered, insecure, pathologically narcissistic, physically and verbally abusive toward her daughters, particularly the more vulnerable Hope.

The most salient aspect of characterization in the novel, however, is the relationship between Faith and Hope. The fact that Faith and Hope are twins serves as a mechanism to suggest alternative life possibilities. The difference in their life situation can be attributed mainly to their different experience in relation to incest, as well as to the fact that Faith is the first born. This latter fact accounts for Faith's feeling of responsibility toward her younger sister. The devastation caused by incest is reflected in the fact that Faith feels responsible for not being able to protect her sister from the consequences of her (Hope's) victimization: "I'm supposed to protect you and look out for you, and you're killing yourself and there's nothing I can do" (169). As the more mature sister, she serves as the voice of reason.

The details given of the immediate context, the home, in which the incest takes place enhances the characterization of the sisters as incest victims. The story presents the home environment as one conducive to the perpetration of incest because of the attributes and behaviors of both parental figures. The stepfather is shown to be an incorrigible victimizer, who has not only committed the incest on Hope, witnessed by Faith, but in addition has made frequent attempts to molest Faith as well: "Papa had tried to reach into her blouse and squeeze her budding breasts, as he had tried so many times before" (86). Faith's reaction, at age fifteen, of defending herself by slashing him with a razor results only in clarifying the role of her mother, Irene, as a silent partner in her own daughter's abuse, as she is more concerned about the welfare of her husband than about that of her daughter. The clarity of the mother's choice leaves Faith with no alternative but to run away, for the third time. Faith, therefore, is herself a survivor of several incest attempts and of the same home environment that permitted her sister's victimization. As the story develops and as time passes, the actions of the main characters indicate clearly that this is a household characterized by multiple sick, codependent, relationships: Faith and her mother, Hope and her mother, Faith and Hope, Irene and her men, even her friend Tina and Irene.

The narrative attempts, with some success, to present a multifaceted picture of Hope, the primary incest victim, by referencing a variety of physical and non-physical attributes. She is presented as "a shade lighter" (13) than her sister, "getting downright skinny" (13), but distinguished from her sister particularly by the difference in educational accomplishment, manifested in the language she uses. This is indicated, somewhat awkwardly, by attributing to her the habit of adding "and stuff" to her sentences. She is also shown to display one of the behaviors which children who have been victims of sexual abuse sometimes exhibit: the mutilation of the pelvic area of her dolls (46). This evidence of the profound psychological damage caused by incest is, however, not developed explicitly in the novel. Instead, the perspectives that her mother and sister have on her are privileged, so that she is represented through their eyes for a large part of the story, not so much as victim, but as sexually precocious, and intentionally promiscuous, particularly with her mother's boyfriends. When Henry asks Faith, "So how many of your mother's boyfriends has Hope screwed now?" Faith answers, "I think this makes three. Four if you count Papa" (42). Thus the two most influential female figures in Hope's life, her mother and her twin sister, who both function in maternal capacities, regard her as a sexual predator instead of primarily as a victim of an incestuous family system.

This negative aspect of Hope's character is supplemented, if not contradicted, by the presentation of another dimension of her personality. She may be a sexually promiscuous, foul-mouthed, drug abuser, but she is more than that in the eyes of some of her familiars. The elderly Mrs. Shelling sees her as an extremely caring individual: "That sister of yours is a gem. I told her she should get a job as a home health aide since she seems to like taking care of people ... It's nice to have someone around who actually cares if you live or die" (83). On the whole, however, the effect of her victimization is accurately represented in the attitude of self-blame, typical of many incest victims, which Hope exhibits in her account of her molestation: "I don't think he even started the whole thing. In fact, I know he didn't. I did" (166).

Faith's narrative perspective plays a critical role in our understanding of, and reaction to, all the characters in the story. For a large part of the novel, the reader is obliged to accept Faith's frequently unsympathetic judgment of her sister. In the end, however, as Faith's consciousness develops, so does her awareness of the reality of her sister's victimization. Faith's voice emerges, therefore, as the voice of reason, of truth, which attempts to counter the distortion in perspective that has been destroying her sister:

> You don't have enough reasoning power to decide to have sex when you're ten. You were a child and he was an adult. He was your parent, for God's sake. It was his responsibility to look out for you, not to take advantage of you. But he was a pedophile. He knew what he was doing. You may have thought it was your idea to kiss him, but he was buttering you up to get to that point. (168)

While the characterization of the sisters contains many elements consistent with their experiences as victims of incest, the relationship between them and their mother often borders on the satirical and does not ring true. The interaction between daughters and mother seems inauthentic. Faith expresses affection and consideration toward her mother, Irene, to the extent of cooking for her and generally pandering to her desires. Irene acts in a protective and nurturing way toward Faith, taking care of her after Hope's betrayal. These actions that speak of familial nurturing and consideration belie the story's reality that Irene did not protect either daughter from being sexually abused by their stepfather, that Irene was a silent partner to the incest and attempted incest of her daughters, and that she continued to have a relationship with Ronald, an abusive, alcoholic man. Indeed, because of the way in which the daughters relate to their mother, Irene emerges as an unrealistically sympathetic character.

Both sisters exhibit characteristics consistent with victims of incest: from Faith's role as a parental child, to Hope's drug abuse, promiscuity, vulnerability, and caring for others. The jealousy that Faith experiences in relation to her twin sister is understandable as is the responsibility she feels as the older twin. Faith's attitude to Hope, untrusting and to some extent jealous of her sister's sexual proclivities, may be interpreted not merely as a consequence of incest, but as a conventional staple of the contemporary genre of the "relationship" narrative, increasingly popular among black American women readers, in which jealousy constitutes an obstacle to the course of true love. This genre presents the black female, even outside the incest experience, ideally as sexually assertive, capable of seducing any available black man, who has no defense against the charms and physical attributes of the black woman.

Coincidentally, therefore, one of the functions characterization and plot serve in this story is evidently to stimulate interest, empathy, and understanding, particularly in Black/African American readers. Black writing, as an indicator of cultural specificity, plays an important role in the narrative, as a factor that contributes directly to the development of character and plot. Literature in general serves as a means of escape for Faith from her intolerable home environment: "Faith had turned to books to escape the nightmare of living with Papa"(99). Yet a mutual interest in black literature establishes a bond between Faith and Henry when they first meet. They are both sensitive to, and knowledgeable about, their African American literary antecedents, particularly the luminaries of the Harlem Renaissance. The significance of this tradition is manifested concretely in the fact that elements of this tradition are literally inscribed in the text of this narrative. This inscription takes the form of excerpts from poems by Claude McKay and Langston Hughes which are quoted and reproduced in the text. Faith, moreover, expresses pride in the fact that she shares a birthday with James Weldon Johnson, while Henry jokingly claims to have been born on Langston Hughes's birthday (101). Both of these central characters, therefore, are firmly grounded in the African American literary tradition. This tradition exists as an element of characterization which, on one hand, establishes this narrative as being sensitive to, contributing to, and continuing that tradition, and, on the other, serves as a unifying bond at the level of relationship between characters. This tradition is thereby validated as essential to strength of character and to human value for persons of African American heritage.

Characterization serves also to deflect attention away from the "unspeakable" aspects of incest and emphasize other plot elements that might stimulate the readers' interest. The introduction of the character of Ann, Faith's friend and business partner, provides an alternative focus of concern — Faith's life outside the family circle as an upwardly mobile black woman and as a professional. The fact that Ann is a lesbian creates another focus of reader attention: Ann's relationship with her partner, Carol. The talk of a possible marriage between Ann and Carol and the secretive plans surrounding the event constitute a subplot that helps to spotlight further the more prominent love relationship in the novel, that between Faith and Henry. The secrecy surrounding the Ann/Carol event is used as a narrative stratagem to prepare for the "romantic" dénouement of the novel.

The central concern of the story, however, is undoubtedly the dilemma of telling. And the differentiation between the sisters serves as a primary mechanism for exploring this dilemma. What unites both sisters, apart from their genetics and early childhood experiences, is an awareness that telling (the truth) is not always a simple matter. The dilemma of telling and the complexity of the consequences of disclosure become significant plot threads throughout the narrative. Thus, the central focus of this incest story as developed from the prologue is not so much on the experience of incest but on the perceptions and responsibility of the 11-year-old witness in relation to disclosure—to tell or not to tell. Within the short space of this prologue, Faith oscillates between the two possibilities: "I wanted to tell, but I didn't really have anything to tell. I mean, I knew something was going on, but I didn't know exactly what" (2). Her stepfather's sly suggestion—"Faith, you don't have to tell your mother everything you know" (4)—exploits the child's vulnerability in confirming her doubts about the necessity for disclosure. He further reveals his desire to manipulate her by the bribe he offers her: "And get yourself whatever you want while you're at the store. I'll tell your mother it's okay" (4). Faith evidently sees through this transparent attempt at manipulation, but her stepfather's words and actions only serve to swing the pendulum in another direction: "Now he went and said that, and that meant I would have to tell Mommy, because if I didn't, we would all be playing another game—one called 'Let's All Hurt Mommy'" (4). Faith's dilemma is further complicated by her situation as a twin and her conception of twinship as a bond too precious to violate: "But if I did tell Mommy I would be telling on Hope, and I never told on Hope and she never told on me" (4).

While at this stage of the story Faith is not presented as a direct victim of incest, she is nevertheless emotionally victimized as a sibling and particularly as a twin. Thus this prologue to the story accurately expresses the dilemma of an incest victim in relation to the sense of responsibility she typically feels toward the "silent" partner in the incest (her mother), as Faith labors under the illusion that her silence is protecting her mother: "[I]f I did tell, Mommy would put Papa out ... But then Mommy would be all sad ... and she probably wouldn't be able to get another man to like her" (5). The most persuasive argument against telling for Faith was the perception of personal responsibility: "And it would be all my fault for telling" (5). This inner conflict adds depth to Faith's character and provides a plot interest that is potentially as engrossing as the consequences of incest.

While incest provides the initial impetus for the dilemma of telling, this dilemma is explored in the story in plot elements unrelated directly to the incest experience. This dilemma is raised for instance by Faith's mother, Miss Irene, in relation to her suspicion that something was going on between her most recent boyfriend, Ronald, and Hope. For Miss Irene, the central question is whether Faith would have told her if she thought or knew about Ronald and Hope sleeping together. Miss Irene's insistence opens the door for Faith to remind her of what had happened before when she (Faith) had told: "It didn't do me any good when I told you before, did it?" (136). For Faith, the past experience made her forever question the utility of telling:

> "What was the use of my telling?" Faith's eyes brimmed with tears.
> "I came and I told. I told and you didn't do anything, Mommy. You let me down and you let Hope down." (136)

The permutations on the dilemma of telling which the story explores through a variety of characters and situations contribute to a correlative exploration of the significance of silence. At the macro level, the novel as printed and voiced narrative, neutralizes and counteracts the silence in which incest is often shrouded. At the level of the novel's content, the plot further examines the characters' attitudes and responses to the admonition to silence. The complex role of silence in the dynamic of incest is presented in the first major flashback of the novel, which appears as an italicized section in the second chapter (42-46). In this scene, the stepfather exercises his control by putting an end to discussion: "*I told you I'm finished talking about it!*" (42). The imposition of silence effectively silences the mother and guarantees and even justifies his position of absolute (masculine) authority. Even the victim, Hope, is initiated into the necessity for silence and becomes terrified at the thought of any voiced communication about her experience: "*There was a look of pure terror on her sister's face. Her eyes were wide and tearful, but they spoke to Faith, pleaded with Faith, 'Please don't ask me about it. Please don't make me talk about it'* (43).

This incest story illustrates the way in which silence functions as an intrinsic part of the incest system. Faith's early experience of telling has thus taught her to doubt the value of disclosure and has encouraged her to silence. She practices the repression of her voice, particularly in relation to countering that of her mother which she knows to be fallacious, since she is not convinced that voicing the truth is likely to produce any effective change: "Faith bit her lips to keep the words from coming out. All you did, she thought dismally, was tear the family apart" (136).

Thus, the process of coming into voice operates as an element of plot development in the narrative. A climax in the action of the novel is reached, therefore, in the heated confrontation of Chapter 9, when the voicing of contrasting

opinions on the perpetrator and the victim brings the conflict between mother and daughters to a head. Miss Irene's
contention that "he was a damn good father" (143) arouses
Faith's ire: "He was a child molester, Mommy. Admit it. Say
it. He was a fucking child molester who was screwing your
eleven-year-old daughter!" (144). Miss Irene's allegation
that Hope "was a little slut, even then" (144) is countered by
Faith's angry riposte:

> "She didn't go to bed with him!" Faith yelled at
> her mother. "He raped her. She was only eleven.
> He raped her. He was a pervert. A child molester.
> You brought a child molester into our house. Our
> family. It wasn't Hope's fault and you know it. It's
> your fault! You let that dirty bastard screw your baby
> daughter and you didn't do anything to stop him.
> Even when you knew! Even when I told!" (144)

This scene emphasizes the fact that the admonition to
silence which is recommended and practiced in many communities encourages the perpetuation of a climate that favors
incest. In the critical scene in which Faith confronts her
mother specifically about revelation of the truth, Miss Irene
gives voice to one of the common attitudes that characterize the incest environment: "Don't you dare air our laundry
in front of strangers!" (146). But even as Faith breaks this
taboo, insisting that she is glad that she told, she still remains
conflicted, questioning the appropriateness of telling: "[I]f
I did the right thing, why am I crying? Why is everyone
crying!" (147). This confrontation and Faith's voicing of the
truth prepares for the dénouement of the novel. In fact, as far
as the development of the incest theme is concerned, from
Faith's perspective there is nothing more to be said. The only
other development in the plot in relation to incest will be the
revelation by Hope of the pain that the incest experience has
caused her.

The motif of "telling" serves also as a mechanism for character differentiation. Faith is not only the person who tells. She is also the listener who can be told the truth. Thus, after Hope is accused by her mother of sleeping with her boyfriend, Ronald, Faith plays the role of mediator who can hear both sides of the story. She is willing, therefore, on Hope's urging, to listen to her sister's account: " 'Go ahead and tell me your side of the story,' Faith answered carefully" (63). The two sisters display contrasting attitudes toward disclosure. This differentiation is explored outside of the main plot focus of incest in a scene where Hope witnesses her friend's husband in a compromising situation with another woman. For Hope, there is no dilemma. She knows what the right thing is to do: "You ain't even married a year yet and you're out here hoing around? Oooh, I'm telling. I'm telling, I'm telling!" (158). And tell she does. This action by Hope is shown to be one that generates admiration (184) and produces a result that is on the whole helpful. The husband, Jason, is impelled to confess his dereliction, and Hope's friend, Susan, is confirmed in her suspicions, is able to express her anger with justification, and has the comfort of knowing she has a reliable and supportive friend in Hope.

The narrative exploits the "telling" motif also to provide a contrast in character between the sisters and to use this contrast effectively to insert a plot complication—an obstacle to the course of true love between Faith and Henry—and at the same time to establish a direct link to the effects of incest on victims: while Faith, the witness and voice, can develop a relatively successful life, Hope, the victim, manifests multiple signs of suffering from the consequences of the incest trauma, in relation to her educational status, her drug use, her promiscuity, and feelings of inadequacy and unworthiness.

This development is effected through another complication in relation to telling in the scene where Hope "confesses" to sleeping with her sister's boyfriend, Henry (206). Her later retraction of the confession (216) paves the way for

Faith to explore the motive behind her sister's lie and this explanation casts light on the damage the incest experience has caused to Hope. Hope's italicized outcry, *"Ain't I worth being the one that's choosed?"* (219), announces the erosion of her self-worth and indicates the immensity of the wound her mother's response to the incest has produced.

Significantly, this poignant moment of the revelation of Hope's pain and vulnerability is not allowed any narrative development. Instead, the news that Irene has had a heart attack immediately displaces the dramatic interest. Incest and its effects play no further part in the narrative. The final chapter introduces us to a Hope who is six months drug free and putting on weight, a Miss Irene who has lost fifty pounds, a family that appears to be harmonious, a surprise marriage proposal by Henry, and a surprise wedding ceremony—in other words, a contrived fairytale ending.

One of the devices employed in this novel to render the unspeakable nature of incest more acceptable for the popular fiction market is the attempt, while providing illustrations of the less palatable aspects of violence which necessarily characterize incest, to introduce and highlight elements of sexuality which may generate their own interest. The story does illustrate that incest is primarily an act of violence and an abuse of power particularly through the characterization of the incest perpetrator as a man given to physical violence against women and children: *"Papa's hand came down across Mommy's face—hard"* (44). This violence is meted out even to the young Faith: *"Faith hadn't realized that she had backed into the hallway until she bumped into Papa, who then knocked her into the wall so hard she saw bright flashes of light dancing in front of her eyes"* (44). The violence practiced by Papa is counterbalanced, however, by the frequency with which sexual elements are highlighted in the narrative. These elements result in shifting the focus away from an incest story to the genre of popular erotic fiction.

The tendency toward highlighting eroticism is exemplified, for instance, in the initial physical description of Faith, which focuses on details that emphasize her sexual attractiveness: "At five feet four inches and 140 pounds, with breasts so firm she seldom wore a bra, Faith had a small waist and a big butt that drove men wild" (9). With this description, interest in her character shifts immediately from her role as witness to incest to that of sexual object in her own right. This displacement of focus is repeated in the linear development of the plot from chapter to chapter. While Chapter 1 sets the mood of a family drama that has to be resolved between twin sisters and their mother, this mood is broken in Chapter 2, which presents a shift in location and in interest. In this chapter, the action moves from the mother's house in the first chapter to a bar and later to a hotel room, which presents a scene of sexual role play between Faith and her boyfriend Henry. The details of their interaction, the explicitly sexual language they use, the specific references to body parts, and the description of their acts of foreplay and copulation are deliberately suggestive to the extent that the whole scene verges on the gratuitously pornographic. Similarly, Chapter 7 presents another erotic interlude (107-12) in which the two lovers play one of their intimate games before discussing the problem of Hope. Chapter 13 (189-93) also is another interlude, less directly erotic, which recounts a role-play scene between Henry and Faith in a restaurant.

The insertion of these scenes raises the question of their function within an incest story. The notion of sex for sex's sake in this story distorts the consideration of incest as primarily an act of violence and misuse of power and invites the suggestion of sexual pleasure as somehow related to incest. The inclusion of gratuitous eroticism in this incest narrative creates a salacious interest that detracts from the tragic aura that so often surrounds the incest experience and the telling of this experience.

The gravity of incest as a personal and social violation is mitigated also by a narration that is not consistently credible. While some elements of the narration are plausible and for that reason provoke interest, others are less convincing, particularly the ending of the story. The narrative effectively conveys the multiple challenges associated with telling and the behavior of Hope as an incest survivor is to a large extent accurately represented. Irene's characterization is a believable reflection of the portrait of the mother in an incest household, but her relationship with her daughters stretches the imagination. Moreover, Henry's gang activity and his subsequent transformation into idealized black successful manhood is definitely romanticized. Similarly, no explanation is provided within the narrative of how and why Faith moved from considering her sister, Hope, as sexually aggressive even as a ten-year-old child, responsible for seducing her stepfather, to defending her as a victim of rape. Hope's situation at the end, well on the way to recovery from her drug addiction, stretches believability, since there is no evidence of her participation in therapy for her incest experience. Twenty years of Irene's blaming her daughter, Hope, for her men leaving her, and characterizing her daughter as a whore all appear to be forgotten. These flaws in plot and character development appear all to be related to a concern with sanitizing the incest story in the interest of popular acceptability.

The aspect of this novel that provides the most convincing substantiation of an authorial attempt to make the incest story acceptable for the popular fiction market is the ending. Indeed, one of the challenges in the narration of this narrative is the preparation of the surprise romantic, unrealistic, *deus ex machina* dénouement. This dénouement is initiated in Chapter 5 through a mysterious telephone call from Ann received by Irene, whose side of the conversation is overheard by Faith. Her discovery that Ann and Carol are getting married is as much a source of astonishment as the news that the wedding is supposed to be kept a secret from her. The question she poses to her mother, "Why does she want to surprise me?" (77), is not answered satisfactorily on this occasion, but creates an opening for another plot interest to be developed and resolved. In the end, the primary characters, including Hope and Irene, are all doing remarkably and inexplicably well. This ending effectively distracts attention from the reality of the devastating consequences of incest and allows the reader to retire from the narrative in the comfortable assurance that everything turns out well in the end.

Thus, this incest story has little, if any, therapeutic value for survivors of incest. The betrayal of the silent partner is for victims one of the most damaging and painful aspects of the incest experience. This story depicts the victims, including the one who escaped (Faith), as continuing to be victims in the way in which they interact with their mother, the silent partner. The mother is never held responsible; no transformation in her thinking occurs; and she makes no apologies for not protecting her daughters. Faith never rejects her mother, despite her expressed love and feeling of responsibility for her twin sister. The characters revert to denial, as if there is nothing abnormal about what has happened. Even Henry's comment, "You and your mom and your sister are the craziest women I've ever met" (111), diminishes the traumatic effect of the damaging mother-daughter dynamics. Most pertinently, telling makes no difference whatsoever. It did not save the victim or dismantle the system. This incest story leaves the incest system firmly in place.

And yet, *I'm Telling* is undoubtedly an incest story, a story constructed about and around incest, and a story that explores, however imperfectly, one of the central dilemmas of the incest experience: to tell or not to tell. Whatever its shortcomings, the novel succeeds in counteracting the taboo and in presenting incest in a format that makes light of the unspeakable and transforms it into popular entertainment.

Chapter Three

FICTIONALIZING THE CLINICAL: *IN MY BEDROOM*

᷍ঌৡ

Donna Hill's *In My Bedroom* may be considered literally as a fictionalized clinical study of incest. The story demonstrates a concern with the accuracy of the representation of the incest experience in relation to the characteristics and behaviors of incest victims and the characteristics of the incest household and of the perpetrator, particularly in the process of recovery for incest survivors. The concern with verisimilitude—conveying the appearance of reality, convincing the reader that the representation is believable and accurate in relation to lived experience—has been an age-old concern of literary (dramatic) production, most notably with the Aristotelian recommendation of respect for the "unity" of action in Greek drama and the development of "realist" and later "naturalist" approaches to the European novel in the nineteenth century, which sought to correlate fiction and pseudo-scientific theories of social life. In response to such a concern, *In My Bedroom* consciously invokes the authority of "science," including documented clinical findings on incest, as the basis for its "fiction," and, in an apparent paradox, presents the incest story as at the same time both fact and fiction. The narration is at pains to construct a picture that can be accepted as the real-life experience of an incest survivor and to attempt to ensure that the depiction of the incest experience in this story is consistent with the findings of "objective" scientific studies and is, therefore, validated internally by the events and characters in the novel and externally by documented clinical practice. This reliance on the clinical is underscored in several ways.

The importance of the clinical is signaled right at the beginning of the text by references in the acknowledgments to a psychotherapist and a psychologist to whom the author expresses a debt of gratitude. The inference to be drawn from this notation is that the content of the narrative—the actions and situations of the characters—has been authenticated by the experience of these clinicians. The privileging of clinical authority is further enhanced in the body of the narrative by the role of one of the primary characters, Dr. Pauline Dennis, who is herself a clinician, a medical doctor, who manages the process of recovery for the primary incest victim. The duality of Pauline's role as both clinician and incest victim serves to enhance her credibility. The authority of the clinical is also invoked at the end of the text by the inclusion of a page of references—published articles and books related to incest. These citations seem to position *In My Bedroom* as not simply a fictional story but also, at least in part, a scholarly enterprise.

The importance attached to the clinical approach is reflected as well in the methodology of story-telling. The writer who is about to embark on the project of fictionalizing incest has to make a variety of decisions in relation to the telling of the story. One such decision relates to narrative perspective and particularly the degree to which, and by what method, the perspective of the victim or survivor should be privileged. Conveying this perspective affects the choice of narrator, most typically, according to narrative convention, either first-person or third. Since personal experience, unlike interpretations and insights, is difficult to challenge, first-person narration permits the illusion of authority and authenticity, despite the narrator's limitations of knowledge and perspective. While third-person narration can impart a certain authoritative objectivity, once the decision has been made, as in this story, not to use the (first-) personal testimonial approach, the persona and the perspective of the third-person narrator are crucial factors in rendering the story plausible and convincing. The authorial desire to convince the reader of the accuracy of the representation of the incest experience results in a narrative that is frequently auto-referential; the third-person narrator often finds it necessary to interpret and explain the significance of narrated behavior or action for the benefit of the reader who, because of the aura of taboo that typically surrounds this topic, may not be sufficiently informed about specific characteristics of the context and consequences of incest. Thus, when Rayne's alternate persona emerges in a session with Pauline asking for a cigarette and insisting on the separation between her and Rayne ("Me and Rayne") (111), and Pauline knows that Rayne does not smoke, the narrator explains: "For the most part, multiple personality was something many psychiatrists read about, but rarely had an opportunity to treat. Splits in personality were triggered by something devastating that the central self cannot handle" (112).

The concern for verisimilitude is reflected also in the formal structure of *In My Bedroom*. On one hand, the novel alludes to the world of the imagination in the use of a poem to launch the story and, on the other, it signals, through its organization, the objectivity of its artificial construction as an incest story. Thus, the incest story is framed by an opening poem and a closing page of references. This combination reinforces the interplay of fiction and clinical accuracy. Even the poem, titled "7:11," attributed to Cece Falls, which is used as a preface to the story, manifests the duality of fact and fiction. This is a stunningly effective poem, accurately described by Hill herself in the acknowledgments as "beautiful and poignant." As a poem, with all the artificiality associated with this form of writing, it is nevertheless designed to create the illusion of authenticity, since the poetic persona who voices the poem appears to be herself an incest survivor. Moreover, this poem raises themes such as the persistence of memory even after twenty-three years, the flashbacks, the disassociation and fragmentation, as well as the difficulty with disclosure, which are typical of the experience of incest (verifiable by clinical practice), and which will all be developed within the body of the story.

Within the outer framework of the poem and the references, the incest story is divided into thirty chapters inside an interior frame of a prologue (1-9) and an epilogue (252-255). The formality of this architecture points to the artificiality of the construction of the narrative. The use of the devices of prologue and epilogue highlights a deliberate arrangement of events and situations in order to separate the temporal context of the main action from the period preceding and subsequent to the action that constitutes the core of the story. This structure emphasizes that the narrative is no mere documentation of happenings but a carefully organized story designed to highlight specific aspects of the problematics of incest.

From the perspective of the structure of the narrative, the prologue plays a crucial role as an exposition, particularly in outlining the themes to be developed and the permutations of the problems to be explored in the body of the story, raising questions, alluding to mystery, and creating suspense. The prologue prepares for the development of the theme of incest by presenting the primary character at a moment of crisis. The prologue introduces the protagonist and the events that immediately precede and explain the situation in which she finds herself in the main part of the story, and also signals some of the narrative challenges faced in the process of telling an incest story. The peculiarities of the protagonist's behavior and the mystery surrounding this behavior function as narrative devices to stimulate interest and create tension. The manipulated desire to obtain an explanation for these unexplained occurrences induces an artificial suspense designed to hold the reader's attention until full revelation is made as the story progresses.

One of the central mysteries to be explored is the personality of the protagonist, Rayne Holland. In the prologue, we meet the protagonist as a grown woman, thirty-five years old, living initially with no consciousness of her problem, with few acknowledged memories of her incest past, with no awareness of her fundamental disorder, and consequently without having taken any steps toward recovery. In other words, as we first meet the protagonist, she is an adult victim of childhood incest. Thus the initial challenge of the narrative is to present an "authentic" portrait of a typical incest survivor. How does such a person present herself? What does she look like? What behavioral traits characterize her? How would we, as readers, as observers, recognize such a person?

The exploration of the incest victim's life as it evolves over time constitutes the primary linear focus of the story's plot. The complexity of the life situations in which Rayne is involved creates additional points of interest which function as subsidiary plot lines in the narrative. Rayne's professional activity as a filmmaker both mirrors and conceals her personal dilemma. Her behavior, thoughts, dreams, affect, actions, and reactions are detailed to present a picture of a tormented and wounded psyche: the victim of a trauma so devastating as to cause her personality to shatter and literally split. The main plot investigates the underlying cause of this trauma as she undergoes therapy in a hospital setting. The narrative immediately exploits a mystery around which the focal tension, the suspense, is built: What is the explanation for Rayne's condition? What caused her suicide attempt?

In My Bedroom is in fact a double incest story built around the convergence of the incest of the central character and the incest of the therapist. Rayne's recovery journey is guided by Dr. Pauline Dennis, whose own experience of being sexually abused as a child and her recovery present a parallel plot line. In addition, there are a significant number of subplots: Rayne's suspicion of her husband's infidelity; her jealousy of Gayle; Gayle's obsession with and jealousy of Rayne; Gayle's relationship with her own husband; the developing relationship between Rayne and Robert; Pauline's experience of incest and the counter-transference that occurs with Rayne. Thus, the incest story seems to be overshadowed by at least two other important stories: two problematic marital relationships and the complex friendship and rivalry between Rayne and Gayle.

Rayne is introduced to the reader in the prologue by a third-person narrator as a highly successful filmmaker engaged in viewing her documentary, *Back When We Were Free*, based on case studies of incest survivors, for which she has already won several awards, including the Independent Film Critics, the Black Filmmakers, and a Sundance. The prologue is at pains to suggest that there is more to her than what she presents to colleagues, friends, and family. No direct link is established at this point between Rayne's professional activity and her personal experience, but the narrator's focus on Rayne's immediate physiological reaction to the viewing of her documentary hints at a mystery in relation to her psychological balance: "A thin sheen of perspiration began to coat her body, beginning at her belly, rising upward to her face then down between thighs" (1). Rayne is presented as being suddenly assailed by an "unknown sense of dread," and she overreacts in paranoid fashion, screaming and running, to the sudden, unexpected touch of a masculine hand on her shoulder. These unexplained overreactions on the part of the protagonist in the prologue represent questions that will be explored and answered in the body of the narrative.

The prologue emphasizes the dimensions of Rayne's personality disorder by describing symptoms that would be typical of such a disorder. The Rayne who appears in the prologue has suffered a mysterious two-day memory loss, when she finds herself at home with her husband, Paul, and her daughter, Desiree. One of Rayne's most agonizing problems is the loss of memory: "She searched her mind, tried to replay all the images and she couldn't remember. Couldn't remember" (3). Later, she finds that something has occurred to spoil the formerly harmonious relationship she had enjoyed with her colleague, Kevin: "What had happened between the two of them? Why couldn't she remember?" (5).

The prologue suggests that memory, voice, and trauma are all intertwined. Memory loss is presented here as a symptom of psychological trauma. Therefore, the recapturing of memory is an indicator of recovery. Thus, completing or reconstructing the narrative of her childhood is as essential for Rayne's recovery as for Pauline's. While the use of a third-person narrator facilitates the reproduction of the voice of Rayne's alternate persona, the motif of voice (and voicelessness) underscores one of the central concerns of this incest story and incest stories in general. In the context of incest, society imposes a restriction on talking about, relating, incest experiences, and voicelessness is often a consequence of the experience. On the other hand, telling (the story) is a mechanism for healing and recovery. Therefore, the textual narration (the telling of this tale) contributes to the breaking of the societal taboo.

The prologue also hints at the manifestation of a problem in the area of trust and intimacy with her best friend, Gayle.

This relationship has its challenges and it is Rayne's inability to confide fully in Gayle that provides the question on which the novel's title is based: "How could she explain what she was uncertain of, talk about what happened in her bedroom?" (7). Both of Gayle's closest intimate relationships, with her husband and her best girl friend, are thus shown to be problematic. This lack of trust is further emphasized when, toward the end of the prologue, we learn that Rayne has found a letter in her husband's suit pocket. This discovery prepares us for another focus of interest in the story.

Rayne's situation, as presented in the prologue, typifies one of the fundamental elements of the incest experience: the silence that characteristically surrounds this taboo, the fear of the effects of disclosure, the difficulty of finding a listening ear, and the communication disconnect that often exists between victim and the community. This disconnect necessarily produces trauma, manifested in behaviors and attitudes that would be, to the initiated, symptomatic of an underlying psychological disorder.

In sum, the prologue introduces a character whose behavior and inner voices suggest an unresolved psychological trauma. The reader is made aware that there is something wrong with Rayne and that the revelation of this mystery will constitute the main line of interest in the narrative. At the same time, however, the prologue, as an element of the narrative structure, invites reflection on a number of aspects of the composition of the narrative which are already directly highlighted or implied. At this early stage of the tale, the incest experience and its after-effects provide the focus of the whole narrative.

While the prologue introduces the major themes and plot lines to be developed in the body of the story, the epilogue offers resolution of all the mysteries presented in the prologue. The epilogue, referring to a date six months after the main action of the story takes place, presents Pauline attending a meeting of a group of incest survivors and introducing herself to the group. This public admission of her problem is clear evidence that Pauline is on the path of healing and recovery. Similarly, the epilogue indicates that Rayne is also firmly on the path of her own rehabilitation since she can now write about praying for the compassion to forgive her father (253). Her stepmother, Edith, is doing well, moving to Louisiana with her sister. Gayle and her husband, James, are on their second honeymoon, talking about having another baby. Robert has made peace with his father, and there is a hint of a possibility of a resumption of a relationship between him and Rayne. The epilogue, therefore, neatly resolves all the challenges faced by the characters and closes the novel with the final notation of Rayne's situation: "She was alone. One with herself. At last" (255).

Within this carefully orchestrated framework, the core incest story evolves. One of the central challenges confronted in the telling of an incest story is the place of the incest in relation to the plot, i.e., the series of events that constitute the primary story line. At what point is the incest incident featured? What prominence is it given? How graphically is it related? Is incest central or is it peripheral? And who tells it? In *In My Bedroom*, the challenges of telling the incest are met through a variety of narrative strategies. These strategies vary because there are two incest victims whose stories need to be told and because the telling of their stories is complicated by the circumstance of their relationship as victim and therapist.

As the novel opens, Rayne's situation as an incest victim is suggested only by allusion, although her illness and recovery will constitute the main plot line of the novel. At this early stage, the focal motif of incest is subtly indicated through Rayne's professional activity, and the narrator takes pains to interpret the social significance of the subject matter of the documentary that she is producing as well as the psychological effect on Rayne: "It was both horrific and emancipating to hear their tales of physical and emotional recovery from society's dirtiest secret" (1). Rayne's work on case studies of incest survivors functions, therefore, as a narrative *mise en abîme* (or story within a story). The subject matter of her documentary, the telling of incest stories, is a reflection of the subject matter of the narrative in which she is the principal case study.

Rayne's telling of her own incest experience occurs in the twelfth of the thirty chapters, as Rayne finally gets the courage to talk about the rape to Pauline. The initial incident occurs when Rayne is six years old, soon after the death of her mother. Her father is shown to be under the influence of alcohol, confused to the point of calling her by her mother's name. The rape itself is described as if by an observer:

> "Da-ddy!" She covered her face with her hands and screamed until her throat was raw, her voice barely audible. Her body quivered helplessly as he spread over her.
> Pain. Pain. Pain like she'd never experienced before ripped through her, ringing her ears, tearing her flesh until everything was black and empty and her body throbbed and burned as if tossed in hot oil.
> When she opened her eyes, she was alone in the dark, afraid to move. The strange stickiness sealing her thighs. (105-6)

Significantly, the incest is not narrated by Rayne in her own voice but in a flashback scene by a third-person narrator. This narrative decision begs the following questions: What is the significance of the narrative technique employed here? Why is Rayne not permitted to tell her own story? To what extent does this third-person narration enhance or mitigate the severity of the rape? By the manipulation of the combination of first and third-person narration and of direct and indirect speech, *In My Bedroom* cleverly presents one of the most common characteristics of the incest experience: the difficulty for victims to talk about, to voice and to give a name to the reality they have lived.

The third-person narrator plays a crucial role in explaining the significance of the characterization in the incest story and in helping the reader to interpret their functions. The third-person narrator adopts the role of clinical expert to explain through the perception of the clinician, Dr. Dennis, the existence of Rayne's alternate persona:

> The more she's listened to this "other Rayne," the more she realized that she was in actuality a rebellious child, the one Rayne had never been allowed to become. She was the one who stomped her foot and said no, had the tantrums, the spontaneity, and the provocativeness. And because the aspects of adolescence and all that went with it had been fractured at such an early age, the two parts that would have made the whole had grown up as separate individuals, appearing and disappearing as the need arose. (232)

This narrator explains that the main characters—Rayne, Gayle, Robert, and Pauline—are all "challenged by a lie, a misconception" (225). The narrator also explains for the benefit of the reader Rayne's place in the structural arrangement of the characters who constitute the story. The basic symbol used by the narrator to explain Rayne's role is that of mirror. As the narrator explicitly observes, Rayne serves as a shattered mirror through which the other characters see themselves: "At the epicenter of them all was Rayne Holland. It was through her shattered image that they had been compelled to see themselves and all their frailties. As she'd traveled along the road to recovery, so did they all" (225).

Through the narrator's eyes, Rayne's incest and the evolution of her story serve as the catalyst, the inspiration and motivation for other people to confront their own demons: Pauline, the therapist, has undisclosed incest and can deal with her own therapeutic issue in the epilogue; Robert, the landscaper—alone, unmarried, and filled with resentment— has abandonment issues with his father, who is described as a strong man for abandoning his family; Gayle, Rayne's best friend, has been emotionally abused by her parents in being always compared to her brother who was killed. Also, she is left full of insecurities, never feels good enough, is jealous of Rayne and wants her husband; Edith, the stepmother ("who'd stood silently by while her father, *her* husband, raped her" (237)), is in an abusive relationship with Rayne's incest perpetrator and is rescued by Rayne in the end.

The third-person narrator who mediates Rayne's story provides the figurative context that a six-year-old would not have had: "To her six-year-old eyes, he appeared like a giant black shadow towering and dangerous, with unimaginable power ..." (104). Equally plausible, however, is for an adult, 35-year-old Rayne to have supplied this context. As Rayne's recovery becomes more grounded, she can begin tentatively to give voice, albeit in very unspecific language, to the reality of the occurrence: "'My ... father ... hurt me,' she said in a whisper, then stronger, more assured" (212). Nothing more explicit is revealed at this point. This is the extent of the telling, even though the narrative, through the mediation of Pauline, insists on the therapeutic value of this pseudo-revelation in moving Rayne from the position of victim to survivor (212). Healing occurs finally only when Rayne is able not just to voice but to name the reality of the incest: "You raped me, Dad-dy," she slung at him. "Over and over again" (241).

The telling of Pauline's incest is effected through two different narrative strategies: indirect free speech and first-person (direct speech) narration. Her first account of the incest is related in indirect (third-person) free speech and the description of the incidents is similarly indirect. She refers to "her uncle who used her body at will" (137) and admits, "She'd never told anyone about what had happened to her as a young girl, not even her therapist. She never even whispered about her uncle's carnal abuse of her young body or his threats to hurt her if she ever told" (138). Her first person account of the incest surfaces in a recording that she had made of a session with Rayne, when the tape continued running without her knowledge. Thus her supervisor, Dr. Howell, is able to use Pauline's own words, in an exercise of a related form of abuse of power by a male, to support Rayne's perpetrator and counteract Pauline's attempt to help Rayne: *"How many nights did I lie awake in bed listening for the footsteps at my door, waiting for my uncle Thomas to appear, whisper things to me that no man should whisper to a child? I know the helplessness"* (197). Only at the very end of the novel is Pauline able finally to admit and name, in her own words, her incest experience and the specific nature of the offence: "My name is ... Pauline Dennis and my uncle raped me when I was nine years old" (252). This echoes Rayne's earlier confrontation of her father and signals a parallel movement toward self-healing.

According to the convention of novelistic production, characterization is one of the primary devices used to render stories believable. Characterization, plot, and theme are intimately interconnected in this novel. The primary characters all demonstrate evidence of fracture and this fragmentation is related in every case to the keeping of secrets: Rayne, Gayle, and Pauline are all keeping secrets; Gayle did not even tell her husband she had a brother; and James has a secret gambling debt which Gayle is not supposed to mention. All have a fear of disclosure. The three primary female characters provide related focal points of interest, converging on the idea of sacrifice, which emerges as an important sub-theme in the novel: What is Pauline willing to risk to save Rayne?

What is Gayle willing to risk to help Rayne? The answer to these questions has to be "Everything." This totality of commitment to healing and to personal integrity lends the novel an epic dimension, investing the characters involved in the confronting of these dilemmas with heroic status.

In *In My Bedroom*, the central character, as a survivor of incest, must demonstrate by her words and actions the typical characteristics of an incest survivor, as documented by clinical practice. Individual character traits, characteristic gestures, words, and expressions, serve as designators of individual identity. Indeed, one of the central concerns of the narrative is to detail many of the effects of incest manifested typically in incest victims: overachievement, image of sexual assertiveness or aggressivity, abnormal fear of males, a need to control, issues of trust, and the fracturing of personality.

The multiplicity of problems that clinical practice associates with incest take shape in the novel mainly through the characterization of Rayne and her relationship to other characters in the novel. Rayne is a case study who manifests many of the attributes of the adult who has experienced incest during childhood. Indeed, Rayne functions initially in the narrative as the primary reader-audience of a number of incest stories. Her reader-response as filmmaker already anticipates that of the reader of the documentary narrative of her own life. Therefore, the narrator communicates directly with the reader in order to explain Rayne's relationship to the other characters and the symbolic significance of her role in relation to the structure of the novel.

Yet, as the focal point of this incest story, Rayne is more than an incest victim. This incest story is not simply Rayne's story; it is also that of her closest associates: her best friend, her doctor, her husband, her father and stepmother, and her possible love interest. As a victim of childhood sexual abuse, Rayne's character is shown to affect her marriage to Paul, her relationship with Pauline, as well as Gayle's relationship with

Rayne's husband, Paul, and with her own husband, James. While the focus is on a single female character, the introduction of the two other women, Pauline and Gayle, broadens the context of incest. Dr. Pauline's own experience of incest serves to intensify the incest motif and open the question of recovery and healing. Furthermore, the characterization of Gayle expands the reader's view of incest in that she provides a contrasting perspective of another black woman who has not suffered incest. Rayne thus becomes the catalyst for healing in a variety of characters: not only Pauline and Gayle, but also Robert and her stepmother, Edith, a victim herself of a related form of abuse by the same perpetrator, Rayne's father.

The main action of the novel (after the prologue) opens with Rayne in the hospital after an abortive suicide attempt. She is in the company of two other important women characters, her doctor Pauline Dennis, and her best friend, Gayle (Johnson) Davis. These characters introduce sub-plots or alternative centers of focus or mystery: Gayle's problematic relationship with Rayne, with Rayne's husband, Paul, and with her own husband, James; Pauline's own secret problem that mirrors that of her patient. We also meet the two main male characters: the menacing figure of Rayne's father, William, married to the ineffectual and abused Edith after the death of Rayne's mother, Carol, and the comforting but enigmatic figure, Robert, who bears his own secret burden of childhood suffering, and whose father is also a patient in the early stages of dementia.

Featuring a meeting between Rayne, Gayle, and Dr. Dennis, the opening scene of the first chapter serves as an exposition in which Gayle acts as a stand-in for the reader, posing the questions that are or should be in the reader's mind, while Dr. Pauline Dennis, an authority figure because of her professional position, provides the necessary clinical explanations. From Pauline we learn that "Rayne's problem dates prior to the deaths of her husband and daughter. Something that was never dealt with. The car accident was only a trigger for her suicide attempt at her father's house" (13). Pauline poses the questions that provide the central dramatic mystery of the narrative and creates a further dramatic interest by her expressed awareness of a special connection between her and her patient:

> Pauline was intrigued by Rayne Holland, intrigued in a way she was not with her other patients. She knew Rayne heard and understood, was aware of the world. Why wouldn't she speak? What had so traumatized her that she'd rather be silent, shrink into a tiny dark corner of her mind to hide? From what? Who? There was something about Rayne, a familiarity of spirit that drew Pauline to her, a part of her that understood the torment and fear. It was if they were joined in some intangible way. (16)

The third-person narration of this scene is interspersed with the italicized manifestations of Rayne's silent persona. The issue of voice, therefore, is foregrounded early in the scene in multiple ways: first, through Rayne's literal voicelessness, the effect of the traumatic losses she has just suffered; second, as a characteristic of Rayne ("She had never been able to express her feelings, the emotions that swirled within her" [12]); third, through Rayne's alternate persona, who supplies the voice that Rayne apparently never had. The voice of this alternate persona develops as a reaction to the implicit futility of talking: "*I don't talk because they can't hear me. They won't hear me, they never have*" [12]. It also forms a counterpoint to the narration conducted by Rayne in her journal, which serves as the outlet for the voice that is apparently silenced: "*They think I don't hear, I don't feel, don't think. It's not true. It isn't. I write it all down in my journal*" [12].

The idea of not being heard and of not being believed is a common experience of incest survivors, as are the suicide attempts, the betrayal of trust, the fear of the dark, control issues, and sexual dysfunction and disassociation during sex: all of which form part of Rayne's "problem." This "problem" manifests itself in her behavior as a wife. The relationship with her husband, Paul, has become strained, even though initially she had been drawn to the gentleness of his voice, which "could almost make her believe that it was safe in the dark" (4). This repetition of a reference to a problem with the dark subtly underlines Rayne's personality disorder, which has begun to manifest itself in sexual dysfunction. Thus the relationship with her husband, whom she had previously considered as a protector against the nameless fears from which she suffered, has deteriorated to the extent that sex, from Paul's point of view, is so unsatisfactory as to threaten the survival of their marriage: "I want us to have a real marriage where I don't feel as if I'm either making love to a corpse or raping some tearful virgin" (4).

This mutually unsatisfactory sexual relationship is developed in later chapters. Rayne's as yet unspecified problem manifests itself in her fear of her secret being revealed to her husband's too knowing eyes. As a result, she begins to hide her nakedness from him: "*But after two months, it was his eyes that caused me to dress in the locked bathroom or in the hallway if they were just getting up. I didn't want him to read my body*" (29). Paul's reaction was to ridicule her apparent prudery, to insist she undress "in front of him—in the light "(30), to rip off her clothes, and to have sex with her despite her opposition. After this marital rape, when she retreats into a safe place within herself to the point where "it wasn't Rayne whose body he was pushing into, tearing into, filling until he flooded her" (31), their daughter, Desiree, is conceived.

Rayne's relationship with her husband serves both to highlight sexual dysfunction as a documented consequence of childhood sexual abuse and to create a subsidiary plot interest in the unasked question: Had Paul been unfaithful? Similarly, Rayne's car accident and subsequent suicide attempt complicate the plot, since these events oblige her to enter an institution of recovery. The institution itself validates the professional arena as essential to recovery, but incest is not suggested as the immediate cause of her need for treatment. Thus, the trauma of Rayne's losing her husband and daughter is added to a scarcely remembered childhood trauma.

Rayne's character is complemented and complicated by an alternate Rayne persona, introduced in the prologue through the use of italics which indicates the presence and dematerialized voice of an otherwise unidentified character who coexists with and within Rayne. This technical device of a typographical change highlights one of the primary focal elements of the plot: the issue of voice. Italics are used consistently throughout the narrative as an indicator of the alternate Rayne persona. A brief, significantly italicized notation, "*I won't scream. I'll be good*" (2), presents very early on the silent voice of this alternate persona, although the third-person narrator does not offer any explanation at this point of the source or significance of the voice. In the opening scene, Rayne's colleague, Kevin, jokingly responds to her exaggerated reaction to his unexpected touch with the comment, "Figured only little kids were afraid of the dark." The narrator provides an explanation for the italicized notation that interrupts the narrative—"*Things happen in the dark*"—in order to clarify the mystery of the italics: "the eerie words she had not spoken came alive in her mind, shouting at her, clawing at her body" [and] "coming from somewhere deep inside her" (2). At the end of the prologue, we find Rayne losing consciousness as a result of being involved in an automobile accident, aware that "*No one could hear her*" (9). This device is used to breach the barrier of voicelessness that exists at the level of Rayne's consciousness and supplement unvoiced elements of her story. Furthermore, this alternate persona, who constitutes in many ways a different character,

and whose difference is conveyed through her visually different voice, brings the character of the protagonist in line with
the experience of many incest survivors.

Without explicit comment from the narrator, this alternate persona is evoked not just by voice but also by gestures
and attitudes uncharacteristic of the surface Rayne. Even in
the prologue, we note that as Rayne admits her fear to Kevin,
she "adjusted her white blouse and buttoned the top button"
(2). In the first chapter, as the hospitalized Rayne listens
to her doctor and her friend discussing her illness as if she
were invisible, Rayne's alternate persona speaks voicelessly
in italics, and Rayne is described as "beginning to unfas-
ten the buttons of her pale peach cotton blouse" (12). This
characteristic tic of unbuttoning her blouse will be repeated
throughout the novel to signal the presence of Rayne's alternate persona.

The existence of Rayne's "other self" (229) is suggested
too by the practice of smoking and other physical gestures
not associated with the conservative Rayne. In one of her ses-
sions with Pauline, Rayne first asks the doctor for a cigarette,
although the Rayne Pauline knew did not smoke. As the
scene unfolds, "Rayne tossed her hair behind her shoulders
in a sultry gesture, brushing the rest away from her face. Her
expression was serene, challenging. The corner of her mouth
curved, almost alluring. Every gesture was intentionally
seductive" (111). The emergence of this sexually provocative
persona is marked also by the use of "a tone Pauline didn't
recognize. The voice was hard with a worldly edge, not the
often timid voice of Rayne. *Her* Rayne" (111). At this point,
"Rayne began to unbutton the top of her dress' (111). Similarly, in one of her conversations with Robert, the gardener
in the hospital whose father is also a patient, as she finds
herself becoming attracted to him, "Suddenly she wanted to
unbutton her blouse." Her unusual reaction prompts Robert
to ask "Are you all right?" Whereupon the alternate persona

surfaces and manifests itself in italics: "*Don't cry, girl,* the voice warned. *Just answer the man*" (130). The story seeks to provide a clear interpretation of this persona. Thus, toward the end of the novel, as Rayne is moving toward awareness and acceptance of her previously fractured personality, she is able to joke with Pauline: "Who do you think was always unbuttoning the blouse? Her?" (231).

The function of the characterization of Rayne's long time friend, Gayle, within the context of childhood sexual abuse, is to provide a privileged though uninformed perspective on Rayne's behavior as an incest victim over time. Gayle is Rayne's intimate friend but lacks the knowledge to interpret the clues she has witnessed over many years. Gayle knows but cannot assess the significance of the fact that Rayne was suddenly sent by her father to live with her Aunt Mae. Consequently, Gayle's interpretation of Rayne's departure does not even consider the possibility of abuse: "She was sure that Edith was jealous of Rayne and her father's closeness" (19). Gayle is aware of Rayne's "aloofness and…sultry, erotic beauty" (19), but makes no connection between these contradictory traits and the possibility of sexual abuse. Gayle can recall an incident on Rayne's seventeenth birthday, when her innocent question to Rayne, "How does it feel being back home?" results in a strange reaction on Rayne's part:

> [H]er eyes sparked with something that momentarily chilled Gayle…. The look that had darkened Rayne's eyes that day in her bedroom so many years ago was the same look she'd seen earlier at the facility. A look of pure unadulterated hatred that almost possessed a life of its own in its raw power. (20)

Only in the temporal present of the story, as Gayle reflects on the past, can she come close to acknowledging "the truth about Rayne, the little things she'd noticed over the years: the days of silence, her irrational fear of the dark, being touched, and ... sometimes it was almost as if the Rayne she thought she knew ... was someone else entirely" (20). Gayle's lack of awareness is typical of friends and acquaintances of incest victims. Like many others, she lacks the information and sensitivity to read the signs. Gayle's character, who envies and sees Rayne as smug and having it all, attests to the "invisibility" of incest survivors.

Rayne's doctor and therapist, Dr. Pauline Dennis, occupies a role that parallels and illuminates that of Rayne, since Pauline's own similar past experience makes her particularly sensitive to Rayne's situation, and unusually protective of her patient. Rayne's abuse is central, but is complicated and intensified by Pauline's situation. Pauline is Rayne's psychotherapist, but also a victim herself of sexual abuse by her uncle. This experience of Pauline's places her in a privileged position, both as therapist and as advocate and protector, sharing in and identifying with the victimization that her patient has undergone but needing as part of her own recovery to exercise control in a context of patriarchal abuse of power, in the case of Rayne's father, William, and her own supervisor at the hospital, Dr. Howell. Pauline listens to, advocates for, and protects Rayne, directly managing the process of her healing. Pauline also functions as a double for Rayne, as yet another alternate persona, and as a sister-in-incest, since her own incest issues are triggered by being Rayne's therapist. Therefore, her interest in Rayne's recovery transcends the limits of pure professionalism. She seems to cross the line and assume a parental role toward her patient. Moreover, Pauline's own healing is intricately linked to that of her patient. Pauline's insistence in moving Rayne away from seeing herself simply as a victim—"You're not a victim, Rayne. You are a survivor" (212)—signals the intention to make this incest story a survival story. With her help, Rayne becomes not only a survivor but someone who contributes to the healing of other people.

Pauline's experience both as an incest survivor and as a medical professional serves to reinforce the notion of the prevalence of incest, of the permutations of male abuse of women, of the fact that the experience of incest is not limited to any socioeconomic, educational or professional group, and that indeed almost anyone we meet in our daily lives could be a survivor. Her experience also highlights the reality that survival takes many forms and operates at different paces for different people.

Robert's character is not directly related to Rayne's incest experience but is used to indicate some aspects of her recovery, since one of the manifestations of her illness has been unsuccessful relationships with the opposite sex. In addition, Robert brings to the foreground the question of race. This aspect of Robert's characterization is to some extent a distraction and adds little to the primary concern of the novel. However, since race occupies such a dominant role in the daily existence of African Americans, a convincing fictional representation of the black experience would inevitably include references to race, as in this story in which most of the primary characters are black. Robert's secret, his pain, is related to the question long unanswered: why did his father abandon the family? The answer comes late in the novel (220) and is given in the context of Robert's father's experience as a black man working in the wheat, corn, and cotton fields in the Mississippi Delta, as well as in the message he passes on about the responsibility of the black man to his son and ultimately to Robert. The peace, the healing, that Robert finally achieves comes with the recognition of himself as a black man: "Finally he understood who *he* was. He'd come from a line of strong, black men" (222).

Like all narratives, the fictional incest story can function as a cautionary tale, conveying important life lessons and messages. As *In My Bedroom* demonstrates, constructing an incest story has its special challenges in relation to the function of the primary incest victim. Here the central focus is a delicate balance between the representation of the enormity of Rayne's suffering and loss and the persistence of the effects of the incest experience. Rayne loses her innocence, her childhood, her mother, her child, her husband, and her sense of self. As an adult woman she is she is fragmented to the point where this fragmentation affects her marriage. The loss and the fragmentation reinforce the fact that incest follows her into her adulthood. Indeed, her father's attempt to abuse her as an adult triggers her attempted suicide and leads her to end up in a mental institution. In detailing these experiences, the story sends a strong message that her strength as a survivor is used as an anchor for the losses and fragmentation that others experience. This story is constructed in such a way as to demonstrate that the kind of strength manifested by Rayne can lead ultimately to the survival and healing of others.

However, the narrative strength of *In My Bedroom* lies in its fidelity to clinical practice in its portrayal of incest survivors. There is no doubt that Rayne and Pauline are realistic representations of incest survivors, as in their suppressed memories and Rayne's sexual dysfunction. Yet one aspect of the story stretches the limit of believability: Rayne's recovery. According to the narrative, she is in therapy for only a short period and "recovers" almost instantly, confronting her perpetrator and rescuing her stepmother. The implication that short-term therapy can make the incest victim as good as new is an attractive one but not at all supported by clinical practice.

The structure of the narrative and the techniques adopted also raise a number of questions. One of the central questions is the extent to which characterization and plot add to the focal concern with incest. For instance, both incest victims are high functioning and occupy a relatively high class position in terms of their careers. Does their class position mitigate or enhance the gravity of the incest experience? Does the introduction of subplots, such as those introduced in the prologue—the physical and psychological trauma of the loss of child and husband in a car accident—divert attention from the incest and thus reduce its impact? What is the effect of all the plot complications—the relationship with Gayle, Gayle's problems, Robert's problems—on the central interest in incest? Do they cloud or mitigate the force of incest?

These aspects of the technical structure of the narrative underscore the problem of constructing and telling an incest story. Incest is clearly the primary catalyst for the basic plot, but the narration cannot support the burden of an exploration focused exclusively on the experience and impact of incest. This novel is to some extent a survivor's "feel-good" story. But the presence of so many other stories within the novel—the double marital situations, the complications in the friendship between Gayle and Rayne—diminishes to some extent the devastation of incest. At the same time, these subsidiary stories make the double incest story more realistic since the accounts of marriage difficulties, abandonment, friendship, and envy all scream that life is happening.

In My Bedroom provides a number of important messages in relation to incest. The narrative affirms the notion of solidarity among women; it reminds us that we may not know who an incest survivor is, what one looks like, or what she does for a living; it certifies that recovery is possible; and, above all, it validates narration (in the form of talking, story-telling, or journaling) as an essential element in total recovery. This story also serves as a vehicle for giving voice to the voiceless as much as any factual account, and the happy ending functions as a message of hope. The narration of *In My Bedroom* invites the cautionary conclusion that recovery from incest does not occur automatically and that for incest victims to recover without professional help is unlikely. Thus, the narrative validates clinical therapy as the primary mechanism for healing.

Chapter Four

INCEST IN THE RAW: *PUSH*

৵৽

*P*ush by Ramona Lofton, writing under the pen name of Sapphire, is not an easy or comfortable novel to read. A story of survival against incredible odds and with no fairy-tale ending, the work is raw in its description of incest and its effects. The story can evoke reactions of horror and disgust but also of fascination, as a result of the shocking experiences of sexual, physical, and emotional abuse and the novel's language, which is uncompromisingly crude in its vocabulary. The characterization of the survivor-narrator, who is physically unattractive, uneducated, foul-mouthed, often offensive and aggressive, and who communicates in a vernacular that shows little concern for, or sensitivity to, political correctness, can also trigger contradictory responses in readers. The narrator's account of her thoughts and experiences does not allow the reader to relax or be entertained. Incest is shown as essentially heinous, repugnant, and capable of provoking extreme emotional reactions in those directly and indirectly involved. In fact, in many respects, *Push* situates itself as a contemporary American tragedy, as profound perhaps in its philosophical and social implications as such classical Greek tragedies as Sophocles's *Oedipus the King* or Seneca's *Phaedra*, and equally capable of stimulating a cathartic purging of the readers' emotions.

In order to tell the incest story, *Push* adopts the narrative voice and perspective of the incest victim and attempts to reproduce the language register that would be consistent with the age, educational level, and class position of the narrator. While, as critics Janice Lee Liddell and Wendy Rountree suggest, there are slippages, in the sense that the narrator's language use may not always be perfectly consistent with her literacy level (spelling, punctuation, and vocabulary may reflect a more sophisticated competence than someone even at an eighth grade level), the perspective of the narrator is ultimately convincing in its tone and language. The novel succeeds in creating the illusion of a narrative voice that is unmediated by a concern for the sensibility of a literary readership unfamiliar with the "reality" of the life and voice of an incest victim drawn from the lowest socioeconomic stratum, for whom the notion of voice is complicated and intensified by her educational situation as an illiterate child and young woman, and for whom the whole world of letters is one from which she is excluded.

The novel is structured visually and materially in such a way as to underscore the documentary reality of the events and actions described and also to extend the significance of the work as more than mere story-telling. The structure of the text emphasizes the implications of the characterization of Precious, who functions as a kind of narrative scapegoat and who incarnates the suffering and failings of a whole community. On her body and on her life is practiced all the abuse in its various forms that a society can heap on its most vulnerable and most undeserving members. The action of the novel covers approximately two critical years in the life of a young incest survivor as she moves with the help of an intervention from victim mode to that of survivor.

References to specific dates, times of day, street names and place names add to the illusion of reality. The novel is divided into four numbered chapters, each of which indicates with precision the time at which the action takes place. In Chapter 1, the narrator-protagonist specifies that she is now sixteen (21) and that the action moves from "Thursday, September 24, 1987" (4) to "Friday, October 16" – "19 (Monday)" (22). In Chapter 2 she is off to her first day at the Alternative School, where she meets her teacher, Miz Rain. The date is again specified, "October 19, 1987" (50). The action moves to "Wednesday, Oct. 21," and covers the month during which she comes to learn the alphabet: "It been a month now" (62). Chapter 3 opens on "January 15, 1988," with the birth of her second child. Since she is involved in keeping a journal, some journal entries carry specific dates. The action moves through "September, 1988," when Precious wins the Literacy Award and moves to a halfway house, to journal entries of "February 1, 1989," when she discovers she is HIV positive. Chapter 4 opens with a journal entry of "2/27/89." Other entries specify "3/6/89," "3/8/89," and "5/3/89." She goes to her first Incest Survivors meeting and speaks about herself in front of the gathering (130), has a counseling session with her mother (131-6), and attends a meeting for HIV positive girls. The action of the novel ends on a Sunday with Precious in a dayroom in Advancement House, holding her son, Abdul, on her lap.

While the action of the plot ends at this point, the text includes another section, entitled "Life Stories," which reproduces the "Class Book" of the reading group, with "original" contributions of two poems by Precious Jones, "My Life" by Rita Romero, "My Younger Years" and "My Grown Up Years" by Rhonda Patrice Johnson (which includes her own incest story of molestation by her brother), "Harlem Butch" by Jermaine Hicks, and a final untitled poem by Precious Jones. The whole text ends with "1991," the date given for the completion of the book project.

These stories at one level emphasize the importance of writing as a therapeutic activity, beneficial in contributing to self-esteem, developing identity and personality, and ultimately ensuring personal empowerment. On another level, the inclusion of these life stories and poems signifies that the incest story is intended as more than an account of Precious's experience. The overall structure imposed on the story sends the message that the problem of Precious's incest is wider than her suffering as an individual, but is related to other forms of abuse, and has implications for an entire community and society.

But this is first and foremost an incest story. Incest is foregrounded and generates all the developments in the plot. The opening sentence of the story brings incest immediately into notice: "I was left back when I was twelve because I had a baby for my fahver" (3). The term "incest" is not mentioned early in the narrative, however. The circumstances as related by the narrator, who initially is not aware of the significance of these circumstances, are left to speak for themselves. Indeed, the narrator does not even know the word, which she confuses with "insect," and is told the difference by one of her classmates when she is about to go to a meeting for incest survivors: " 'So, what's the big deal insect, incest? I say.' 'One's where your parents molest you, the other is like a roach or bugs,' Bunny say" (123). When Precious finds herself in Harlem Hospital at age twelve after the birth of her first child and is interviewed by the nurse, Miss Butter, the answers she gives to the nurse's questions tell their own story, with no need for narrative commentary:

> "Father," she say. "What's your daddy's name?"
> "Carl Kenwood Jones, born in the Bronx."
> She say, "What's the baby's father's name?"

I say, "Carl Kenwood Jones, born in the same Bronx."
She quiet quiet. (12)

The timing of the revelation of explicit details of the first incest experience is arranged to create suspense in the story. While the narrative reveals right from the start that incest has occurred, the precise circumstances are not described until much later. Indeed, the incest incident that results in impregnation would have occurred years after the first incident. Precious's mother relates her daughter's first incest experience, which Precious could not have recalled:

> So he on me. Then he reach over to Precious! Start wif his finger between her legs. I say Carl what you doing! He say shut your big ass up! This is good for her. Then he git off me, take off her Pampers and try to stick his thing in Precious. You know what trip me out is it almost can go in Precious! I think she some kinda freak baby then. I say stop Carl stop! I want him on *me*! (136)

The complicity of her mother adds another dimension to the sexual abuse inflicted on Precious. Her mother's admission to the counselor, Ms. Weiss, about the first incident, serves as an external authentication of Precious's narrative and reinforces Precious's authority and reliability as a trustworthy narrator. Remembering herself at age seven, Precious's account presents incest by her father as ongoing and constant. The sparseness of her description intensifies the horror of the experience: "Seven, he on me almost every night. First it's just in my mouth. Then it's more more. He is intercoursing me" (39).

Incest in *Push* is not restricted to father-daughter rape. The tragic dimension of the incest is amplified when it becomes clear that Precious is forced to endure sexual violation at the hands of her mother:

I feel Mama's hand between my legs, moving up my thigh. Her hand stop, she getting ready to pinch me if I move. I just lay still, keep my eyes close. I can tell Mama's other hand between her legs now 'cause the smell fill room. Mama can't fit into bathtub no more. Go sleep, go sleep, go to *sleep*, I tells myself. Mama's hand creepy spider, up my legs, in my pussy. God please! Thank you god as I fall asleep. (21)

The unimaginably traumatizing effect of this molestation is reflected in the fact that Precious's sense of security is completely demolished and the incest experience with her mother becomes one of her nightmares: "I am choking between her legs A HUH A HUH. She is smelling big woman smell. She say suck it, lick me Precious" (59).

Incest in *Push* is shown to be compounded by other forms of abuse. In addition to the sexual molestation, Precious is forced to endure a continuous stream of verbal and physical abuse by her mother: "I don't wanna stand here 'n hear Mama call me slut. Holler 'n shout on me all day like she did the last time. Slut! Nasty ass tramp!" (9). Precious is accustomed to having her mother refer to her as "Miss Hot-to-Trot" and "Jezebel ass" (19). The physical abuse by her mother is described with a non-judgmental objectivity on the part of the narrator which adds to the impact of the abuse: "Pain hit me again, then *she* hit me. I'm on the floor groaning, 'Mommy please, Mommy please, please Mommy! Mommy! Mommy! MOMMY!' Then she KICK me side of my face!" (9). This mixture of physical and verbal abuse becomes intensified after Carl leaves:

About three months after baby born, I'm still twelve when all this happen, Mama slap me. HARD. Then she pick up cast-iron skillet, thank god it was no hot grease in it, and she hit me so hard on back I fall on floor. Then she kick me in ribs. Then she say, "Thank you Miz Claireece Precious Jones for fucking my husband you nasty little slut!" I feel like I'm gonna die, can't breathe, from where I have baby start to hurt.

"Fat cunt bucket slut! Nigger pig bitch! He done quit me! He done left me 'cause of you." (19)

The reality of incest in this story is pushed to the level of extreme offensiveness. Precious is sexually abused by her father and her mother, and the incest is accompanied by the verbal and emotional abuse of her mother. Also, the abuse perpetrated by her mother includes forcing Precious into overeating and creating the conditions that result in Precious's becoming a compulsive over-eater. The dramatic scene recounted when Precious was twelve does not end with the verbal and physical abuse. The scene continues with Mama demanding that Precious spend two hours in the kitchen fixing a dinner of "collard greens and ham hocks, corn bread, fried apple pies, and macaroni 'n cheese" (19) for her mother, who then insists that Precious eat, although she clearly states "I'm not hungry" (20). As their interaction continues, Precious describes herself: "Eating, first 'cause she make me, beat me if I don't, then eating hoping pain in my neck back go away. I keep eating till the pain, the gray TV light, and Mama is a blur" (21). The scene ends with further sexual molestation, with her mother's hands between Precious's legs.

The impact of incest on Precious is intensified by the combination of sexual, verbal, and physical abuse that she suffers but also by a crippling form of emotional abuse. Her emotional security is constantly undermined by the accumulation of neglect and lack of demonstrable maternal affection. She is further emotionally victimized by an uncaring mother and saddled with blame even though Precious is just an innocent child. Thus, her tears on giving birth to an "ugly baby" (18) are not simply at the sight of the baby but more tellingly, "I crying for me who no one never hold before" (18).

Yet this story devotes very little attention to Precious's mother's story. All that we are told is that Precious's father, Carl, was her first and only lover and that she had been with him since she was sixteen (86). Precious does wonder "what kinda story Mama got to do me like she do" (96). But no information is given to account for the mother's pathology and to shed light on the factors that may have contributed to such extremities of depravity.

Therefore, this story is more concerned with the experience and perspective of Precious, particularly in the development of her awareness as an incest survivor to the point where she becomes aware that she is not alone, than on elements that might explain the specific abuse perpetrated by either her father or her mother. Focusing on Precious's evolution, the story follows her growing awareness that incest crosses socioeconomic as well as racial lines. Before Precious attends her first "Incest Survivors" meeting, one could have drawn the conclusion, and certainly Precious was under the impression, that incest was restricted to people of color in the inner city. At that meeting, however, Precious meets survivors that are in other socioeconomic categories and learns about the pervasiveness of the incest experience:

> Listen to girl rape by brother, listen to old woman rape by her father; don't remember till he die when she is 65 years old. Girls, old women, white women, lotta white women. Girl's younger sister murdered by the *cult*? Jewish girl, we had money on Long Island (like Westchester), my father was a prominent child psychiatrist. It started when I was about nine years old. (130)

The inclusion of this Incest Survivors scene validates the crosscultural and socioeconomic continuum of the incest phenomenon. Before this scene, the reader could have concluded that incest is a function of poverty and race. The references to survivors from the white middle-class rectifies this impression. As the Incest Survivors group becomes a part of Precious's story, the individual incest story becomes part of a larger narrative in which all incest survivors are involved.

The larger narrative of incest is recounted through the variety of characters presented in the novel. The primary and secondary characters in *Push* are drawn to present a typical picture of the context within which sexual abuse takes place. Of central importance are the characters who form part of the immediate incest household: father, mother, and victim. In addition, there are ancillary characters who help to perpetuate and intensify the abuse: school and social service personnel. There are also the characters who represent possibilities of intervention and hope: the "angels" met along the way, the interveners and the mentors: the EMS worker, Ms. Rain, and Nurse Butter. There are characters who appear as symbols of guidance and hope, such as Louis Farrakhan, Langston Hughes, Alice Walker and, not least, the group of peers who find themselves similarly abused, abandoned, ignored, and rejected by society.

The most comprehensively drawn character is of course the narrator, Claireece Precious Jones, whose ability to share openly her thoughts and experiences gives the reader a privileged insight into her character. Her honesty and sincerity create a lens of sympathy, even empathy, that obliges the reader to accept her view of her victimization and of the other characters with whom she interacts. The multiplicity of suffering and abuse that this protagonist has to endure and survive—the incestuous rape by her father, the equally incestuous sexual molestation by her mother, instances of physical, verbal, and emotional abuse, societal neglect, child motherhood, the birthing of a Mongoloid child, and being infected with HIV from her father—adds to the dimension of this novel as a late twentieth century tragedy. The protagonist is made to suffer abuse and neglect not only from her father and her mother but also from the sociopolitical system in which she lives (educational administrators, teachers, social service workers). The descriptions of varieties of sexual, emotional, physical, and verbal abuse conducted without commentary from the narrator, who is also the victim, serve to underscore the protagonist's innocence and to accentuate her role as a scapegoat.

The story is built around and narrated by a character who, despite her educational shortcomings, can address the reader-audience with a self-deprecating but unapologetic frankness that is curiously endearing. Claireece Precious Jones does not explain the significance of or make excuses for her unattractive physical appearance, particularly her size: "I'm big, five feet nine-ten, I weigh over two hundred pounds" (6). When she finds herself at age 12 in the hospital when her first baby was born, she states further: "I'm tall. I jus' know I'm over two hundred 'cause the needle on the scale in the bathroom stop there it don't can go no further. Last time they want to weigh me at school I say no. Why for, I know I'm fat" (11). This unapologetic, almost naïve acceptance of what many would consider the unacceptable, makes her sympathetic but also invests her with a nobility of character curiously at odds with her social situation. She incarnates many of the characteristic effects of incest: self-hatred, mutilation, hatred of her self-image, as well as other behaviors, such as compulsive over-eating, that are common among incest survivors.

The narrative does not paint Precious's father, Carl Kenwood Jones, in any detail. He is presented simply as an incest perpetrator who is known by the bare facts given of his name and particularly through his daughter's reports of his rape of her and the testimony of his wife. He is someone whom his daughter can recall in these terms: "Daddy put his pee-pee smelling thing in my mouth, my pussy, but never hold me" (18) and "Got to where he jus' come in my room any ole time, not jus' night. He climb on me. Shut up! he say. He slap my ass, You wide as the Mississippi, don't tell me a little bit of dick hurt you heifer" (24). With these accounts, there is no need for detailed character portrayal.

The story allows Precious's mother, Mary L. Johnston, to reveal herself similarly through her actions and words. Through the eyes of her daughter-narrator, she is a grotesque figure in her physical appearance: "She take up half the couch, her arms seems like giant arms, her legs which she always got cocked open seem like ugly tree logs" (20). In addition, her daughter consistently describes her as smelling bad. The grotesqueness of her physical appearance is matched by the depravity of her conduct toward her daughter: a combination of emotional, verbal, physical, and sexual abuse that she constantly dispenses. Precious's mother has a lot in common with Irene, the mother of Hope and Faith in *I'm Telling*. They both exhibit the same narcissism, denial, and rejection of their daughters. However, Precious's mother is not just a silent partner; she is also a co-perpetrator who witnesses Precious's initial molestation when she is an infant in pampers, who even at that stage chooses her man over her daughter by breast-feeding him instead of her baby.

The account of Precious's reaction to her mother's abuse of her is realistic, that is, in line with the reactions typically reported by incest survivors, unlike that of Hope and Faith to Irene's abuse in *I'm Telling*. From the very beginning, Precious demonstrates the complexity of the emotional links that are bound to exist between a child and her abusive mother. Internalized at age sixteen and repressed for years, Precious's rage is now close to the surface: "My hand slip down in the dishwasher, grab the butcher knife. She bedda not hit me, I ain' lyin'! If she hit me I will stab her ass to def, you hear me" (11). Despite this rage, the mother-daughter bond is still very strong and

Precious finds it difficult to maintain consistently an attitude of rejection. As she admits, "I hate my muver sometimes. She is ugly I think sometime" (14). This ambivalence is a realistic portrayal of the attitude of many incest survivors toward the mother who has never protected them from molestation or defended them when the incest was discovered.

Through its presentation of secondary characters, the story provides insights into Precious's world view, her emotional needs, and her system of value, either by Precious's reading of these characters or by her reaction to them. The introduction of the EMS worker, for instance, is important since he serves as an incarnation of the goodness Precious associates with God: "And always after that I look for someone with his face and eyes in Spanish peoples. He coffee-cream color, good hair. I remember that. God. I think he was god. No man was never nice like that to me before" (11). This Latino male is definitely one of her angels, someone who encourages her to "push" (16).

Similarly, the description of the nurse whom Precious later dubs Miss Butter subtly signals the concerns of people of color living in a society dominated by race and the complexities associated with the "N" word in the Black American community: "This nurse slim butter-color woman. She lighter than some Spanish womens but I know she black. I can tell. It's something about being a nigger ain't color" (11). This nurse distinguishes herself by the comment she makes when conducting the intake interview. When she learns that Precious's father and her baby's father is the same person, she expresses sympathy for Precious by saying simply "Shame, thas a shame" (12) and by asking the question "Was you ever, I mean did you ever get to be a chile?" (13). Later, after the Down's syndrome baby is brought to Precious for the first time, Nurse Butter's expression of sympathy and support goes even further:

Nurse Butter hike herself up on side of bed. She
tryin' to hole me in her arms. I don't want that.
She touch side of my face. "I'm so sorry, Ms
Jones, so *so* sorry." I try to turn away from her
Mississippi self but she *in* the bed now pulling
my chest and shoulders into her arms. I can smell
her lotion smell and Juicy Fruit gum breath. I feel
warm kindness from her I never feel from Mama
and I start to cry. (18)

Through Nurse Butter, the reader is given insight into the
immensity of the deprivation of maternal affection and
support from which Precious has suffered.

Ms. Rain functions as Precious's principal mentor and
guide not only in bringing her to literacy but also in exposing
her to ways of thinking that run counter to the internalized
lessons of the incest household in which she was primarily
socialized. We learn from her self-introduction to the class
that she is born in California, her favorite color is purple, and
she sings well (43). Her appearance is not detailed. All we
learn at the first class is that "She dark, got nice face, big eyes,
and hair like I already said" (40). These sparse details mark
her as different and not part of the stereotypical cultural
environment that Precious expects of inner-city New York.

Ms. Rain presents two characteristics that force Precious
to re-examine her previously held judgments of people: her
hair and her lesbianism. Miz Rain's character is developed
first in relation to her physical appearance: she has "long
dreadlocky hair" (39). This physical marker is significant in
that it validates a standard of beauty and of character which
contradicts the value system of the macro-society that has
contributed to Precious's devaluation, exploitation, and abuse.
Precious's statement to Nurse Butter that since joining Ms.
Rain's class "I don't feel shamed" (76) indicates how therapeutic the relationship with Ms. Rain is for her since there

is nothing to indicate that Precious would have moved from shame to no shame without Ms. Rain's intervention.

Ms. Rain helps Precious develop a more balanced social and political consciousness. She acts as a foil for Precious's naïve admiration of Louis Farrakhan, the minister and leader of the Nation of Islam, who has enjoyed substantial popularity among large segments of the African American community in New York: "Miz Rain say Farrakhan is jive anti-Semitic, homophobe fool" (74). Farrakan's alleged homophobia provides the opportunity for Precious to develop a more critical attitude to Farrakhan: "Ms Rain tell me I don't like homosexuals she guess I don't like her 'cause she one. I was shocked as shit. Then I jus' shut up. Too bad about Farrakhan" (81).

The story uses Ms. Rain's literacy class as a mechanism for introducing all the characters who comprise Precious's support group for recovery, the description of whom sheds light on Precious's value system, particularly in relation to race, color, class, beauty, and sexuality. Rhonda Patrice Johnson is a Jamaican, described as a "big redbone girl ... Rhonda big, taller than me, light skin but it don't do nuffin' for her. She ugly, got big lips, pig nose, she fat fat and her hair rusty color but short short" (43). Rita Romero is described as a "skinny light-skin Spanish girl" (44). Jo Ann is the "loud bug-out girl who find my notebook" (43). There is Consuelo Montenegro, the "brown-skin Spanish girl" (43), "pretty Spanish girl, coffee-cream color wit long ol' good hair" (45). Jermaine's sexuality (she is dressed in a "boy suit") is suggested right from the beginning. : "We about the same color but I think thas all we got the same. I is *all* girl" (44).

These characters are essential to the incest story in that they constitute a group of young women who in normal circumstances, because of their differences of race and culture, would not have shared social intimacy. Thus their inclusion expands our comprehension of the perhaps under-reported effects of incest. One of the most painful consequences of

Precious's situation of living in an incest household has been the social and emotional isolation. These characters with whom Precious interacts both highlight this isolation and help to demolish it. They help Precious to feel she is no longer alone. As she puts it, "When I hear Rhonda's story, Rita Romero's story, I know I not the worse off. Rita's daddy kill her mother in front of her eyes ... Then Rhonda's brother raping her since she was a chile, her mother fine out and put Rhonda, not brother, out" (94). Similarly, even though the women that comprise the Survivors of Incest Anonymous group are not described in detail, they serve an important function in contributing to Precious's (and the reader's) understanding about incest: "All kinda women here. Princess girls, some fat girls, old women, young women. One thing we got in common, no *the* thing, is we was rape" (130).

The sense of isolation experienced by Precious before she establishes social contacts outside the incest household is related to another feature of the incest experience: the unreliability and fragmentation of the memory of the incest victim. Incest tends to repress memory, to relegate memory to the realm of the unvoiced. Through this disorder of memory, the experience of incest discourages expression and militates against the coherence associated with narrative construction. The action of the novel becomes a convincing recreation of the incest experience in that it is built around reconstituted, obsessive memories, particularly those of sexual and other abuse.

The frequent intrusion of memory into the narrative highlights a peculiarity of the incest experience: the omnipresence of the past even when specific memories are forgotten or denied, or exist below the level of consciousness and resist attempts at retrieval. The narrator oscillates between a contradictory present of pain and hope and a past of horrific, painful, humiliating experiences. In the present of her second pregnancy, as Precious is standing at the sink washing dishes with her mother calling her name, she flashes back to the last time she was pregnant four years earlier and standing at the sink, when she ends up being kicked by her mother and taken to the hospital (9).

The reproduction of obsessive memories of abuse in combination with continuing painful experiences in the present is used to simulate the sensation, frequently reported by incest victims, of being in a nightmarish vortex from which there is no escape. The story thus records this fusion of past and present:

> For past couple of weeks or so, ever since white bitch Lichenstein kick me outta school shit, 1983 and 1987, twelve years old and sixteen years old, first baby and this one coming, all been getting mixed up in my head. Mama jus' hit me wif fryin' pan? Baby, brand-new and wrapped in white blankets, or fat and dead eyed lying in crib at my grandmother's house. Everything seem like clothes in washing machine at laundry mat— round 'round, up 'n down. (22)

Since she is the narrator, Precious's conception of memory is crucial to the function of this incest story as an account of a journey from voiceless to voice. For Precious, memory constitutes a voice that has not reached the surface, like a tune in the head that no one can hear or, as she explains more graphically, "a TV set wif no picture" (112). The influence of memory is not entirely negative, however. The memory of her first experience of hearing of the need to push creates hope: "I woke up remembering the last time I pushed" (16). This memory enables her to internalize an important life lesson that will prove ultimately to be transformative in her survival and success. The voicing of memory is an important step in recovery: "Ms Rain always saying write remember write remember" (115). Memory cannot be divorced from the story-telling that is associated with writing.

The voicing of this insight occurs toward the end of the narrative. However, one of the fundamental concerns throughout the novel is to reproduce as realistically as possible the voice of an incest survivor. This concern highlights the significance of voice in the context of incest typically. The societal taboo with which the very term incest is invested involves both suppression and repression of voice. Incest carries with it a social interdiction: society appears to promote the view that the experience must not be talked about and that the very mention of the experience should be suppressed. In addition, the victim is often enjoined not to tell by the perpetrator and because of this injunction, and the multiple fears of the consequences of telling, represses her voice. Since the victim cannot voice or reveal the truth about her experience which is an important component of her developing identity, the truth about her self—her being or her identity—is concealed. The combination of voice suppression and repression amounts to a veritable erasure of identity.

In acknowledgment of and in response to such a concern, this novel traces the process by which an incest survivor, whose voice and identity at the beginning are repressed and suppressed, develops a voice and assumes an identity. The first-person narration effectively transmits and translates the problems of voice with which this protagonist is confronted. The novel as a whole, by the linguistic register it adopts and by particular references within the story, provides examples of, and validation for, different manifestations of voice: orality and all forms of writing, including journaling and poetry.

A notable strength of this narrative lies in the reproduction of a voice that paradoxically because it exists outside of the margins of social acceptability is freed of the linguistic inhibitions that would normally accompany conventional linguistic practice. Thus, the lexicon that typifies this voice has no awareness of or concern for political correctness. The result is an expression that is shockingly crude and raw, but which gives the impression of communicating an unvarnished truth.

The desire to express herself is one of which the narrator is frequently conscious. She is painfully aware of this desire which manifests itself in the form of repression. For instance, in class with a teacher whom she likes, Mr. Wicher, she experiences the tension between desire and repression: "I wish I could tell him about all the pages being the same but I can't" (6). A similar tension occurs in her interview at school with the social worker, Mrs. Lichenstein: "What my muver gon' do I want to say. What is she gonna do? But I don't say that" (8). Precious details the process by which repression of voice develops within the school environment: "Kinnergarden and first grade I don't talk, they laff at that.... Secon' grade they laffes at HOW I talk. So I stop talking" (36).

The narrator is aware at some level that voice is a manifestation of existence. The tension she experiences translates an unexpressed belief that to speak is to exist. The desire for expression is therefore a desire to demonstrate her existence in the face particularly of an uncaring white world:

> "I wanna say I am somebody. I wanna say it on subway, TV, movie, LOUD. I see pink faces in suits look over top of my head. I watch myself disappear in their eyes, their tesses. I talk loud but still I don't exist." (31)

Manifested throughout the story in the frequent repetition of the phrase "I wanna say," Precious's vocal repression is related in part to the learned fear of the consequences of expression. The fear of physical violence sometimes keeps her from voicing her thoughts and feelings. When the doorbell rings as the social worker, Mrs Lichenstein, comes to visit her at home, this fear results in Precious's silence: "My muver jump in and say, 'Press LISTEN stupid!' I wanna say

I ain' stupid but I know I am so I don't say nothin', 'cause also I don't want her to go hit me" (14). Similarly, the fear of physical abuse added to the sexual abuse itself reduces her to silence and reinforces her conviction of powerlessness in the face of her father's abuse: "I wanna scream, Oh shut up! Nigger, how you gonna marry me and you is my daddy. I'm your daughter, fucking me illegal. But I keep my mouf shut so's the fucking don't turn into a beating" (24).

The tension between expression and repression is manifested also at the physiological level. Sexual abuse of a child sometimes produces a paradoxical reaction that adds to the confusion and conflict in the mind of the victim: the body reacts despite the mind's rejection of the abuse, so that the expression of the body is in direct conflict with the desire of the mind. Thus Precious's desire for expression is embroiled in the conflict that arises in her being from the paradox of the incestuous sexual experience during which she has no control over her body that reacts despite the rejection of her mind: "My clit swell up I think Daddy. Daddy sick me, *disgust* me, but still he sex me up" (111). Indeed, it seems at times as if the reaction of her body contradicts and represses her internal voice: "Say you love it! I wanna say I DON'T. I wanna say I'm a chile. But my pussy popping like grease in frying pan" (111). The awareness of her powerlessness to control her body's reactions increases her self-hatred: "My body not mine, I hate it coming" (111). The shame produced by this apparent betrayal of her own body in being orgasmic in the midst of an experience that is disgusting and humiliating is another inexpressibly painful effect of incest which Precious shares with other victims.

In Ms. Rain's class, Precious's exposure to a group of her "peers" stimulates her awareness of how repressed her voice has become. She finds the courage to begin to express herself despite her fears: "Miz Rain look at me. I'm the only one haven't spoken. I wanna say something but don't know how. I'm not use to talkin'" (48).

The tension between the desire for expression and repression is presented as a function of Precious's emotional dependence on her mother. Her journey to self-affirmation and emotional growth takes the form of opposition to her mother and specifically of expressing to her mother, and naming, the truth of the experience she has had with her father: "I do tell her one thing as I going down the stairs. I say: 'Nigger rape me. I not steal shit fat bitch your husband RAPE me RAPE ME!'" (74).

Expression evidently validates existence. It is the sign of emotional health and of self-worth. In the Incest Survivors' meeting, when Precious begins to give voice to her incest experience and name the reality that she has lived, her emotional recovery is assured: " 'I was rape by my father. And beat.' No one is talking except me. 'Mama push my head down in her ...' I can't talk no more"(130).

Push consistently establishes a correlation between expression and existence. Precious's identity, her existence as a person, is almost completely dependent on her ability to give expression to her experience. The account of the experience of incest which she provides is certainly individual in that the story focuses on the perception of one person. However, the effect of this individual experience is shown to have implications of a general human problem faced by many persons, geographies, and cultures: the threatened loss of identity. For Precious, being violated by her father drives her to crave a form of suicide—the dissolution of her corporeal identity. This suicidal desire is expressed in metaphorical terms by Precious: "Carl is the night and I disappear in it" (18).

One of the most deleterious consequences of incest is the threat it poses to self-worth, self-hood, and identity. The tragic nature of Precious's situation is aggravated by the fact that society, by ignoring and devaluing people like her, contributes to the erasure of her identity. She is painfully aware of her virtual non-existence:

> I big, I talk, I eats, I cooks, I laugh, watch TV, do
> what my muver say. But I can see when the picture
> come back I don't exist. Don't nobody want me.
> Don't nobody need me. I know who I am. I know
> who they say I am—vampire sucking the system's
> blood. Ugly black grease to be wipe away, punish,
> kilt, changed, finded a job for. (31)

This devaluation of her person is reflected in the notes made by her social worker who wants Precious to be a "home attendant" and not to go to school for her G.E.D. and possibly on to college (119).

Precious recognizes that her identity and existence are threatened not only because of her experience of incest but also because of her condition as a poor, uneducated black girl. She questions why no one called the police on her father when she reported him as the father of her first child at age twelve (125). In fact, she finds it difficult not to attribute her multiple victimizations to her racial situation. Her individual experience is linked to issues of race in the U.S in the forms of internalized racism and racist words and actions.

Thus, Precious's experience of sexual abuse by her father is related to the wider social problem of relationships between Blacks and Whites in the U.S. The importance of this problem is underlined by the persona of Louis Farrakhan, the leader of the Nation of Islam, who operates as a powerful symbol in the novel. The model of black manhood and fatherhood for Precious, Farrakhan's persona serves to counter the contrasting lived reality projected by her real-life father. She sees Farrakhan as "a *real* man, who don't fuck his daughter, fuck children" (58). Hardly surprising, therefore, is that Precious's admiration and respect for Farrakhan is translated into naming her son "Louis" (67). Farrakhan helps to politicize Precious to the point where she can place her father's actions in an historical perspective and understand through the lens of her interpretation of Farrakhan's philosophy the significance of her father's conduct toward her in the context of the past and present history of Blacks in the U.S.:

> First thing I see when I wake up is picture of Farrakhan's face on the wall. I love him. He is against crack addicts and crackers. Crackers is the cause of everything bad. It why my father ack like he do. He has forgot he is the Original Man! So he fuck me, fuck me, beat me, have a chile by me. (34)

Through Farrakhan, as Precious grows in social and political consciousness, she is able not only to find a vocabulary for her abuse but also to begin to see the wider sociopolitical significance of this abuse: "I think I was rape. I think what my fahver do is what Farrakhan said the white man did to the black woman" (69).

This correlation between the individual experience of incest and the wider concept of the rape of black women plays an important role in the development of Precious's personhood. Ms. Rain's reinforcement of Farrakhan's perspective as internalized by Precious expands the significance of the incest story. Incest becomes more than an individual or even a family problem. It is a manifestation of a societal malaise that has its roots in the history on which the U.S. was built: the abuse, violation, and rape of Blacks by Whites. Thus, even though Ms. Rain's view of Farrakhan is not as uncritical as that of Precious, ["Miz Rain say Farrakhan is jive anti-Semitic, homophobe fool" (74)], Farrakhan's ideological perspective is still reinforced by her: "Miz Rain say we is a nation of raped children, that the black man in America today is the product of rape" (69).

The political consciousness that forms part of Precious's accession to personal dignity is related to the ideology that underpins the narrative as a whole. This ideology of the need for Black survival through education, self-expression, and self-empowerment is reflected in the telling of the story. Indeed, one of the most significant aspects of this narrative is the self-consciousness that it manifests, through its narrator, of its own production as a story. Consequently, early in the narration the narrator establishes the conditions of her situation as story-teller:

> Sure you can do anything when you talking or writing, it's not like living when you can only do what you doing. Some people tell a story 'n it don't make no sense or be true. But I'm gonna try to make sense and tell the truth, else what's the fucking use? (3-4)

Conditions of narration may be artificially mediated by a series of masked identities and hidden narrators. Yet the ostensible concern is with coherence and with "factual" accuracy as the narration affects to transcribe the innermost thoughts of the narrator, to follow the unfiltered stream of her consciousness, however crude. As the putative narrator of her own story, Precious must choose the narrative elements—events, descriptions, conversations, characters—that would best meet the conditions she has set. This, of course, an illusion, since the narrator, Precious, is a creation of the author, Sapphire, whose *nom de plume* masks the "real-life" identity of Ramona Lofton.

From the very first page, the narrator introduces herself as a story-teller, addressing her oral narrative to an explicit "you":

> My name is Claireece Precious Jones. I don't
> know why I'm telling you that. Guess 'cause I don't
> know whether it's even a story or why I'm talking';
> whether I'm gonna start from the beginning or
> right from here or two weeks from now. (3)

This is a conscious and self-conscious narration sensitive to the audience and aware of some of the challenges of narrative construction. The illusion of orality is sustained by the reproduction of the vocabulary typical of urban youth of the hip hop generation, particularly in the liberal use of "motherfucker" and "bitch," as well as terms such as "ass," "coon," "cunt," "fuck," "hoe," "pussy," "nigger," and "shit."

This narrative self-consciousness is related to an awareness of the purpose personal stories serve in relation to the development of empathy. The narrator is aware that the story explains the person, and that stories enable audiences and readers to understand and empathize with others. In moving toward forgiveness of her mother, Precious can speculate on her mother's story which would have had to be tragic for her mother to act the way she does and model the empathy that readers could also feel both for her and for her mother: "I cry for Mama what kinda story Mama got to do me like she do?" (96).

The self-consciousness of the narration is most clearly manifested in the fact that the plot of the novel resolves itself in a significant dénouement: the production of what will be the ideal book—the collection of the life stories of all the abused young women: "Favorite book? Maybe it's our book, the big book with all our stories in it" (108).

Individual stories, including that of the narrator, are part of the larger narrative that includes this book, which serves as a metaphor for the lives of many women. In this respect, the story projects itself explicitly as a "message" novel. Its purpose is overtly didactic and the message is directly contained in the title, which forms a running theme throughout the novel. It is explicitly related to the action women need to take for successful birthing, particularly in relation to handling labor pains. Precious's first experience of the need for pushing occurs in a suggestion from the Spanish EMS worker who responds to the 9-1-1 call made when her mother's physical violence triggers her labor: "He say, 'Precious, it's almost here. I want you to push, you hear me momi, when that shit hit you again, go with it and push, Preshecita. *Push.*' And I did" (10). A variation of these words returns to her in dream, as she goes to sleep thinking of having the opportunity to go to the Alternative: "Push, Precious, you gonna hafta *push*" (16).

The significance of this term is extended to signal the effort a victim needs to exert to contribute to her own survival and recovery. The need for this effort is emphasized even in relation to the acquisition of literacy. In an interview with Ms. Rain, who is trying to teach Precious to recognize the letters of the alphabet and begin to read, Precious manages to conquer the fear that threatens to paralyze her and admit to Miz Rain that "the pages look alike to me" (54). Miz Rain uses the same term, "push," to indicate the effort Precious needs to apply: "I want you to try, push yourself Precious, go for it" (54). The same term is employed by the teacher as she tries to motivate the whole class: "Write what's on your mind, push yourself to see the letters that represent the words you're thinking" (61). Later, when further tragedy hits Precious and she discovers she is HIV positive, and Ms. Rain is still encouraging Precious to write, Precious screams at Ms. Rain out of frustration and finally admits how tired she is. Ms Rain insists, however, on the need for persistence: " 'I know you are but you can't stop now Precious, you gotta push.' And I do" (97).

Precious's lived experience of the concrete result of pushing through the pain of giving birth has the greatest meaning for her. Pushing becomes more than a metaphor for her. When she is urged to construct the fantasy of her life, the contrast between such a fantasy and the "reality" of her experience still results in appreciation of the beautiful product that emerges after the pain and the pushing of giving birth: "I would be tight pussy girl no stretch marks and torn pussy from babies's head bust me open. That HURT. Hours hours push push push! Then he out, beautiful. Jus' a beautiful baby" (114).

Through Precious's testimony and the documentation of her progress in the world of literacy, the story asserts the fundamental virtue of education, of reading and writing. *Push* affirms the therapeutic value of journal writing and the power of life-story writing, the writing of survivors' stories, for incest survivors. As has been intimated earlier, however, this story is more than the account of an individual's experience with incest. The story is profoundly autoreferential in that it demonstrates internally and externally the value of writing. Writing exists everywhere in the text. The whole story is in effect the written transcription of the voice of the narrator. This story traces the trajectory of Precious, who has suffered extreme abuse in many forms, as she tries to survive and is enabled to attain self-affirmation and self-expression. She is guided in this process directly by Ms. Rain: "If you just sit there the river gonna rise up drown you! Writing could be the boat carry you to the other side" (97). And the text gives specific illustrations of the struggles of a learner-writer, with misspellings, erasures, and corrections.

The narrative further reinforces the value of writing by venturing into the territory of literary criticism in relation to the roles of author and reader: "The author has a message and the reader's job is to decode that message as thoroughly as possible. A good reader is like a detective, she say, looking for clues in the text" (108). It even includes guidelines for writing poetry: "Ms Rain say don't always rhyme, stretch for words to fall like drops of rain, snowflakes" (109). Writing is a powerful metaphor: a weapon and mechanism for defense as well as a vehicle (along with education and reading) for liberation and emancipation.

Above all, however, *Push* functions as a vehicle to affirm and inscribe the essential value of black writing and writers. The value attached to black writing is evident in that the list of books Precious keeps in her bookcase all pay tribute to black writers and leaders (80). The inscription of black literature is manifested directly in the multiple references to Langston Hughes's home and his "Mother to Son" poem, reproduced in its entirety in the body of the story, and to Alice Walker's *The Color Purple*. One of the highest points of Precious's life is spending a night in the Langston Hughes house (80). Hughes's Harlem home is the concrete site of salvation for Precious, the place to which she aspires and eventually escapes from her parents' and society's abuse and neglect, and the place where she finds healing and solace as a writer. Thus, Langston Hughes functions in the story as a symbol of hope for Precious. The influence exerted in the course of the story by black writers presents a strong argument that Precious is saved by black writing.

The story also affirms the therapeutic value of fictional incest stories for survivors, and Alice Walker's *The Color Purple*, which Precious reads at school, is the primary model for the black incest story. Her discussion of that novel with Ms. Rain results in the expression of contrasting views on "realism" and "reality." As the incest survivor and as the narrator of her own incest story, Precious's opinion prevails as she dismisses the "IZM" stuff. The point at issue is the "fairy tale ending" (83) of *The Color Purple*, which will be discussed in a later chapter. What is significant in the context of *Push* is that this discussion goes to the root of the challenge of writing an incest story and particularly the issue of where and how to end it. Precious, fictional character that she is, although masked as a first-person narrator of her own "real" experience of incest, insists that the optimistic ending has its virtues: "I would say, well shit like that can be true. Life can work out for the best sometimes" (83). *The Color Purple* serves as a model for the dénouement of the plot of *Push*. The optimistic ending of *The Color Purple* foreshadows the equally and deliberately optimistic ending of *Push*. Despite the disclosure that Precious's father, Carl, has died of AIDS and the confirmation that Precious is HIV positive, Precious moves toward acceptance of herself and the conditions and experiences of her life and turns her focus on the present as thankfully and joyfully she reads a story to her son.

Ostensibly a story of incest in the raw, *Push* effectively exploits incest to explore an issue of urgent concern to Black Americans—the plight of the black underclass in urban communities. Horrific as it is at the personal level, Precious's experience is related to a wider social problem that affects a number of young women, particularly in "inner city" communities, who are challenged by a combination of factors: societal neglect and indifference, stereotyping, institutionalized racism and the internalization of white supremacist ideology, and patriarchy. Thus while incest is central in the story, racism seems to be equally central, in that *Push* is more than an incest story. It is also a story about racism, colorism, homophobia, and classism. While the narrator-protagonist embodies and dramatizes the situation of many urban youth, the novel makes a strong statement about literacy as the most effective element for the survival and success of black urban youth. Incest is the optic that sheds light on the wider social, cultural, and political problems that black communities face, including abject poverty and the failures of the social system. Incest is also the optic that provides a viable solution.

However, is Precious's remarkable survival and recovery as much a fairy-tale as Celie's acquisition of education and self-esteem in *The Color Purple*? On the surface, the brutality of the abuse, the rawness of the language, and the depth of the poverty serve to camouflage the fairy-tale nature of Precious's rehabilitation—her ability to be a good mother, the "quantum leap" of her remarkable educational attainment, and her determination to continue against all odds. Not that such an outcome is not possible. It is every bit as possible as Celie's story. Nevertheless, this outcome brings into question the idealistic elements of most incest stories. Are the stories of those we do not usually hear, the stories of those who do not survive, physically, mentally, emotionally, or spiritually, any more realistic than a story such as *Push*?

Chapter Five

SPIRITUALIZING INCEST:
THE COLOR PURPLE

&0-<6

Alice Walker's *The Color Purple* has achieved the status of a classic through its appeal as an inspirational fantasy to hundreds of thousands of readers, particularly women in the United States. This appeal was heightened when the story was adapted for the big screen under the direction of Stephen Spielberg (1985), popularly considered as one of the elite group of contemporary filmmakers, and won critical recognition in the form of eleven Oscar nominations. The novel's 2005 reformulation as a Broadway musical play has only served to swell the numbers of its fans and audience. In fact, the success of these different adaptations underlines the power of the fundamental narrative which relates the triumph of the spirit of a woman over the most challenging of life situations: early loss of father, lack of maternal protection, childhood sexual abuse, forced motherhood, loss of children, separation from her sister, physical abuse, backbreaking physical labor in virtual enslavement, regular marital rape, emotional and verbal abuse, and even abandonment by her lover. This story documents this triumph in its many manifestations from Celie's early childhood experiences to her emergence as a woman of immense, almost superhuman, dignity and worth. The story also traces the triumph of other women as they survive and transcend different forms of abuse at the hands of men and by a patriarchal society.

The story does not attempt to offer an explanation for incest or for the sexual, physical, verbal, and emotional abuse perpetrated on innocent and powerless children and women. Rather, it seems to adopt the position that child-hood sexual abuse is inexplicable at the purely human level and represents a deviation from divine purpose and from the spirituality with which human beings are naturally endowed. As Celie understands from Shug, "Incest part of the devil's plan" (138). The story conveys a fundamental belief that the explanation for incest and other forms of abuse against the weak lies in the separation of man from his spiritual purpose and that the solution and recovery for victims are to be found in recognition and application of the power of the human spirit, through which the "God" idea is manifested, and in the efficacy of prayer.

The spiritual focus of this novel is underscored in the authorial dedication: the novel is dedicated "To the Spirit: Without whose assistance/Neither this book/ Nor I/ Would have been/ Written." This dedication reveals the author's belief system, a form of spiritualism that is less restricted and less anthropomorphic in its concept of a supreme creative being than that proposed in conventional organized Christianity. The use of the term "written" in its application both to the book and to the author suggests also the author's belief that human existence, her very being, may be considered as the narrative manifestation of a creative inspiration. In this context, writing is, in its essence, an act of creation. There is no essential difference between the birth and life of the author and the birth and life of the novel she has written. The source of creation is in each case identical.

The Color Purple clearly situates itself as an account of a spiritual journey—Celie's quest to establish a workable relationship with a "God" of her understanding. This relationship is conducted through verbal communication in the form of letters. It is a one-way communication, since the response by this God is not verbal. This response is manifested in the changing circumstances of Celie's life and in the insights she documents as she reacts to these circumstances. The narrative traces the complexity of this evolving relationship and Celie's struggles to develop a concept of God which validates her person and her life situation and to reconcile the new God idea with the experience of victimization that seems to be condoned by the God of her old belief system. Thus, in developing a new concept of God, she has to reject the concept she had inherited through socialization in an oppressively patriarchal society. In the cultural context (Black, African-American, Southern, Baptist) in which this novel is set, God represents the ultimate authority with whom a personal relationship may be established.

The evolution of Celie's spiritual awakening is conducted through the use of a letter-writing format that permits access to what passes for the private thoughts of the letter-writers. The letter format presupposes a limited and privileged communication, essentially private. There are two main letter-writers in the novel: Celie and Nettie. But for the most part the written communication is not read by either addressee. This correspondence is a device by which the narration is conducted: Celie tells her own story ostensibly to God and to Nettie, but in reality to the reader; Nettie tells her story and the story of Celie's children ostensibly to Celie, but in effect to the reader.

In this case, this format is a story-telling and novelistic device, because the final product is published and potentially accessible to anyone. The reader and the addressee are not in real terms the same. In the epistolary format in general, two elements are of particular significance: the addressee and the signatory. Factors such as language register, choice of lexicon, choice of detail, and degree of explicitness are determined by the relationship that exists between narrative persona (letter-writer and signatory) and the addressee, and by the characteristics of both.

The epistolary format adopted for this story complicates the notion of a taboo associated with incest. In the context of North America, incest is still taboo in human societal terms. The incest system relies on silence, or on non-disclosure, for its continuation. It is in the perpetrator's interest to impose silence on all the parties involved, the mother of the household and the victim. This narrative is structured as a series of letters, for the most part written, often not sent, not delivered, not received, and not read by the addressee. As the primary narrator addresses her communication to God, the force of the taboo associated with the incest system remains intact. However, the form of communication employed in this story extends incest beyond the frame of the concerns of human society and introduces a spiritual element into the communication which subverts the societal convention. Paradoxically, this narrative succeeds in dismantling the taboo precisely through the structure it adopts.

The external structure of the text is simple: it opens with the line, *"You better never tell nobody but God. It'd kill your mammy"* (11), which provides the justification and stimulus for the first letter addressed to God, which initiates the letter-writing that develops into the correspondence (the Celie and Nettie letters) that comprises the body of the narrative; the communications and the entire text close with the word "Amen," the term that denotes the end of the prayer within the Judeo-Christian formal religious tradition. This structure clearly marks the text as an extended prayer, as a supplication to God.

The mandate to secrecy with which the story opens is the cultural norm of the community within which the primary action of the novel is situated. God is the confidant of last resort in cases where revelation is frowned upon. For instance, when Squeak is sexually abused by her uncle and shame inhibits her from talking about the incident, Shug employs the same terminology to urge her to speak: "Yeah, say Shug, if you can't tell us, who you gon tell, God?" (95). The whole narrative is a response to an order intended to prohibit disclosure but which ironically produces a communication that will be beneficial and ultimately liberating for the narrator.

The story does not follow the novelistic convention of dividing the action into chapters. It is structured internally around a series of letters addressed to God ("Dear God"), each of which forms what could be considered as a "chapter." The first series of "Dear God" letters constitutes the first third of the novel (up to p. 112), until Celie's "Dear God" letter introduces and includes a "Dear Celie" letter. This insertion prepares us for the second series of letters, a new movement in the narrative characterized by the "Dear Celie" series (119-132), which culminates in a "Dearest Celie" letter (131). The "Dear God" series resumes briefly (134-138), to introduce in the same fashion as before another "Dear Celie" sequence (138-162). A climax occurs at the end of that section with the announcement by Nettie that "Pa is not our pa!" (162), which produces the shortest letter/chapter of the novel, addressed to "Dear God," but in which Celie reaches the conclusion that the addressee of her communication "must be sleep" (163). This observation introduces another movement in the narrative as the addressee of the letter changes: Celie's communication is now addressed directly to "Dear Nettie" (164), which provokes responses addressed to "Dear Celie" or "Dearest Celie" (168-174). Celie makes it clear that the change in addressee is deliberate: "Dear Nettie, I don't write to God no more, I write to you" (175). This segment ends when Celie signs off "Amen" (179, 185, 187, 201) and Nettie responds with a couple of letters (202-214). The remainder of the narrative consists of letters to Nettie (215-225, 229-241, 245-248) alternating with letters from Nettie to "Dearest Celie" (226-8) and "Dear Celie" (242-244). The final letter (249-251) is addressed to "Dear God. Dear stars, dear trees, dear sky, dear peoples. Dear Everything. Dear God."

These movements represent significant developments in the central plot line: the relationship between Celie and her God. As indicated by the salutation and the name of the addressee, these developments are underscored by similar changes in the signature part of the letter. For instance, no signatures appear for Celie's communications in the first part of the novel. Yet Nettie's letters are all signed, as befitting a writer who is more educated, more traveled, and more in tune with the conventions of letter-writing, and the terms she uses as she signs off convey her emotional and spiritual attitudes. Therefore, Nettie signs her letters to Celie, "Your loving sister, Nettie" (112, 150), "love, Nettie" (119, 121), "Your sister, Nettie" (120, 124, 127, 130, 143, 147, 157, 159, 174), "Your everloving sister, Nettie" (133), "God bless you, Nettie" (154), "Your devoted Sister, Nettie" (162), "Pray for us, Nettie" (169), and "Your Sister in Sorrow, Nettie" (171). The first time Celie uses a sign-off, she does not use her name, only "Amen" (179). The use of "Amen" marks the narrator's acknowledgement that her communication is definitely a form of prayer. With this acknowledgement comes the development of a new sense of personal and social identity, so that she can sign off by adding a full address that includes the name of her new business to the recognition of her relationship to her sister and her God: "Amen, Your Sister, Celie, Folkpants, Unlimited. Sugar Avery Drive, Memphis, Tennessee" (192). The recognition of this double relationship is indicated by her continuing to use the "Amen" sign-off (198, 201) and beginning to add "Your sister, Celie" (194,

224, 225, 241, 248), which develops into "Your loving sister, Celie" (217), and later "Pray for me, Your sister, Celie" (221), until the final letter that ends with a simple "Amen" (251). This sign-off not only closes the narration, but confirms the narrative as a spiritual communication.

This structure clearly establishes this story as a communication with God, in other words, as a prayer, a spiritual supplication framed explicitly by "Dear God" and "Amen." Also clear is that this communication is stimulated as a response to the injunction laid down in the first line of the text, italicized for emphasis: *"You better never tell nobody but God. It'd kill your mammy"* (11). This threat to the mother is a strategy adopted by perpetrators frequently reported in real-life incest stories. The opening injunction to silence is significant in a variety of ways. Neither the identity nor the gender of the voice is indicated textually, although this voice is recognizable as that of the "father." These words convey a not so subtle threat—a threat of reprisal, of punishment—as well as an attempt at manipulation, transferring responsibility for her mother's life on to an innocent and powerless child. The deliberate use of the ultimate authority figure in a community that has internalized Christian socialization makes the threat even more potent. The family into which Celie is born and in which she is raised is a Christian family, and she and her sister have developed a concept of a God whose judgment is to be feared. Talking or writing to this God is not an easy undertaking for Celie, as is explained much later by her sister, Nettie:

> I remember you said your life made you feel so ashamed you couldn't even talk about it to God, you had to write it, bad as you thought your writing was. Well, now I know what you meant. And whether God will read letters or no, I know you will go on writing them; which is guidance

enough for me. Anyway, when I don't write to you
I feel as bad as I do when I don't pray, locked up in
myself and choking on my own heart. (122)

Nettie's comment helps us to understand the way in which
the form of this novel, a written text in epistolary format, is
justified internally (that is, as part of the logic of characterization); the narrator needs and desires to tell God, but shame
inhibits her orality; writing letters to God is the only recourse
available. The irony is that the narrator obeys the injunction
literally, and through her obedience, her submission to this
authoritative voice, gains eventual release and victory.

The construction of this story clearly indicates that the
spiritual itinerary on which Celie embarks is triggered by the
first incest experience. Particularly this experience, in light of
the terms of the injunction imposed on her, makes her seek
spiritual explanations. The experience has evidently shaken the
foundation of her self-image, as the elision of "I am" implies
(11): "~~I am~~ I have always been a good girl" (11). The elision
indicates her attempt to tell the truth, and the truth is that
she now has doubts about her moral and spiritual worth.

Two accounts of early incest experiences are given by
Celie, the first in a letter written directly to God, yet both
referring to a time when she was around fourteen. In the
first account, she gives her age as fourteen and the incident
as having taken place "last spring" (11). The familial conditions in which this incident takes place are clear: the desire
on the part of the male perpetrator to exert control over the
women in his household; her mother's unavailability as a
sexual object for the male; the absence of the mother; and
the parentification of the child victim. All these conditions
are typical of the incest household:

> Last spring after little Lucious come I heard
> them fussing. He was pulling on her arm. She say

It too soon, Fonso, I ain't well. Finally he leave
her alone. A week go by, he pulling on her arm
again. She say Naw, I ain't gonna. Can't you see
I'm already half dead, an all these children.
   She went to visit her sister doctor over Macon.
Left me to see after the others. He never had a
kine word to say to me. Just say You gonna do
what your mammy wouldn't. First he put his thing
up against my hip and sort of wiggle it around.
Then he grab hold my titties. Then he push his
thing inside my pussy. When that hurt, I cry. He
start to choke me, saying You better shut up and
git used to it. (11)

The second account of an early incest act is narrated as part
of a letter to God, but as a recollection of a conversation with
Shug. In this account, Celie states that the incest occurred
when she "was just going on fourteen" (108), which invites
the speculation that this may be a description of the same
incident described earlier:

But one time when mama not at home, he come.
Told me he want me to trim his hair. He bring the
scissors and comb and brush and a stool. While
I trim his hair he look at me funny. He a little
nervous too, but I don't know why, till he grab
hold of me and cram me up tween his legs. (108)

The two accounts given of what could very well be the
same incest act, though not contradictory, are not consistent
in the details given. No explanation is given for this apparent discrepancy, but the reader is left to conclude that both
reports are accurate. The question that arises from this dis-
cordance in narration is: to what extent does the discrepancy
cast doubt on the narrator's credibility? Curiously, not at
all. The different descriptions may be accounts of two different incidents, or different perspectives on the same inci-

dent, but there is no suggestion of dishonesty or deception on the part of the narrator. The narrator's life situation, the fact that she has been an innocent victim, abused from her earliest years, and deprived of formal education, marks her as someone who deserves the reader's sympathy. The language with which she is provided for the narration is crude, unsophisticated, unpolished, unrefined, and appropriate for someone of Celie's level of literacy and social conditioning. Her knowledge is restricted: the information she has about her own children is limited (12, 13) and much later the truth is revealed (161). However, these limitations serve paradoxically to confirm her sincerity and her intention to be honest. Moreover, the fact that her communication is addressed to God invests it with an aura of veracity—literally of honest-to-God truth—and endows her with a sense of integrity and credibility as a narrator.

This novel's incest appears to be related to a fundamental belief, accepted by members of the society in which the action of the novel takes place, in the identification of God as the ultimate male figure. The society not only believes in but practices and tries to enforce conformity to the acceptance of male power. The parallelism between God and male domination is emphasized continually throughout the narrative. Unlike the pantheistic spirituality that the narrator eventually embraces, organized Christianity is a mechanism for maintaining and reinforcing a patriarchal belief system.

The ironic association between incestuous violation and the patriarchy of the organized religion to which Celie has been exposed is highlighted in the explanation she gives of the children born from her rapes. Her response to her mother is significant:

> She ast me bout the first one Whose it is? I say God's. I don't know no other man or what else to say ....

Finally she ast Where is it?
I say God took it.
He took it. He took it while I was sleeping. Kilt
it out there in the woods. Kill this one too, if he
can. (12)

In Celie's childish imagination, there is no real difference between the Christian God and her "father." Both are commanding, oppressive figures, exercising total power over her life.

The story illustrates that constant attempts are made to convince Celie that "God" supports the desires and interests of the males in the community. Celie's evolution into infertility transforms her into a desirable object for irresponsible male sexual desire, since there are no consequences in terms of child-production. This new condition is explained by her Pa as a condition imposed by God: "God done fixed her. You can do everything just like you want to and she ain't gonna make you feed it or clothe it" (18). This explanation reinforces the parallelism between the God concept and patriarchy, since the God invoked here is evidently looking after the interests of the men.

Thus the story, which is that of Celie's recovery from the trauma of incest, begins with the act of writing to God. This act allows Celie to be completely honest and to unleash and confront the demons within her. Another stage in the story and in her recovery process is reached when she decides not to write to God anymore but to her sister Nettie, because of the awareness that "the God I been praying and writing to is a man. And act just like all the other mens I know. Trifling, forgetful and lowdown" (175). Celie articulates her conception of God more clearly in the ensuing discussion with Shug. When she describes this God as "He big and old and tall and graybearded and white. He wear white robes and go barefooted" (176), Shug can help her to develop another concept of God: "I think it pisses God off if you walk by the color purple in a field somewhere and don't notice it" (178). This discussion helps to open Celie's eyes to the reality that the concept she had of God was based on the internalization of an image constructed by man, particularly white man.

The relationship between incest and Celie's development of a new concept of spirituality is demonstrated in her struggle to contest ideas she receives even from Shug whom she admires, respects, and loves. The first time incest is mentioned explicitly in the novel is as part of a comment attributed to Shug: "Shug say children got by incest turn into dunces. Incest part of the devil's plan" (138). Celie has to resist this interpretation of her experience. Her emerging new spirituality offers more optimistic possibilities.

Walker uses incest in this story to provide an extreme illustration of a fundamental and widespread problem experienced by women generally: their relative lack of power in a world dominated by male desire and male wishes. The world in which women live is one in which there is constant danger of various forms of abuse by males. The community in which Celie finds herself is one in which males are supposed to hold absolute power over females. Incest is just one manifestation of the abuse of power by males, so that there are frequent examples of various forms of male violence against women. Pa's words to Celie, "You gonna do what your mammy wouldn't" (11), establishes a motive for the incest: the child as sexual stand-in for the mother or wife and her transformation, after her mother's death, into the role of parentified child, fetching water from the well, preparing meals, getting the children ready for school, and even child-bearing (12).

A woman's lack of power is illustrated in the mixture of physical and sexual abuse that Celie suffers at the hands of her stepfather. Celie's Pa has exclusive rights to her attention, does not condone any supposed opposition to his desires, and meets any real or imagined threat to his absolute control with violence: "He beat me today cause he say I winked at a boy in church" (15). The "he say" is significant since it implies that his word, his perception, is all that counts. The later revelation that "Pa is not our pa" (161) carries the implication that the incest suffered by Celie is less shameful because the perpetrator was not a blood relation. Her incest becomes just another rape, less abhorrent than father-daughter incest, and almost acceptable in this community in which women (particularly black women) have little or no rights.

The story is set in the South, at a period when black males, who saw themselves as oppressed by white society (Celie's own father, as she discovers much later, had been lynched), and are becoming oppressors themselves by exerting their limited power in the only place they can with impunity—against women and children. The females in the novel are all described and treated as property. Celie's wishes or feelings are never considered. As Pa informs Mr. _____, "I can let you have Celie" (17). Male power in this community takes the form of control over the access to education for women. Celie is deprived of the opportunity for education, and taken out of school by her perpetrator the first time she becomes pregnant after the incest: "The first time I got big Pa took me out of school. He never care that I love it" (19).

Male dominance in this black community is maintained through the indoctrination of male children into the system of male privilege and authority. Young Blacks are evidently socialized to abuse women physically, as well as verbally and emotionally. The abuse Mr._____'s twelve-year-old son, Harpo, wreaks on Celie on her wedding day is in effect condoned, since it results in no consequences for the youngster: "He pick up a rock and laid my head open. The blood run all down tween my breasts. His daddy say Don't *do* that! But that's all he say"(21). Harpo is indoctrinated by his father into the culture of inflicting physical abuse on women: "Harpo ast his daddy why he beat me. Mr._____ say, Cause she my wife" (30). When Harpo complains about not being able to make Sofia do what he wants, his father's advice is to hit her: "Wives is like children. You have to let 'em know who got the upper hand. Nothing can do that better than a good sound beating" (42). Celie's advice to Harpo that he should beat his wife (43) is an indication that abuse begets abuse and that some women contribute to the continuation of systems of male dominance. When Sofia confronts Celie about this advice, Celie confesses her jealousy of Sofia's power and her sense of self and admits that her advice was a manifestation of her own feelings of powerlessness: "I say it cause I'm jealous of you. I say it cause you do what I can't" (46).

The system of male dominance is shown to be responsible for the acts of incest committed on women and Celie is not the only victim of sexual abuse by a male family member. Squeak, who lives with Harpo after Sofia is imprisoned, is raped by her white uncle:

> He took my hat off, say Squeak. Told me to undo my dress. She drop her head, put her face in her hands.
> My God, say Odessa, and he your uncle.
> He say if he was my uncle he wouldn't do it to me. That be a sin. But this just little fornication. Everybody guilty of that. (95)

This patriarchal system manifests itself in other forms of sexual molestation. Albert, Celie's husband, although he may not be an incest perpetrator, is still a sexual predator in that he attempts to seduce and rape Nettie, his young sister-in-law:

> After a while I had to rest, and that's when he got down from his horse and started to try to kiss me, and drag me back in the woods.

Well, I started to fight him, and with God's
help, I hurt him bad enough to make him let me
alone. (119)

The career of the principal incest perpetrator, Pa, serves as
a reminder of the apparent injustice of this patriarchal system.
In spite of his patently abhorrent character and actions, he
seems to prosper: he acquires the land of Celie's lynched
father, has several wives, experiences and expresses no guilt
or remorse, and dies apparently happy in the act of copulat-
ing with his last, teenage (eighteen-year-old) wife. While the
manner of his death may be interpreted as a form of comeup-
pance, the relative "success" of the most despicable black male
character in the story is one of the most curious features in an
incest story that in all other respects privileges the voices and
perspectives of women and supports their liberation.

The physical, economic, emotional, and spiritual oppression and liberation of women is the most dominant theme in
The Color Purple, developed around the initial focus of incest.
The relationships among women are complex because of
their different positions in relation to self-liberation. Shug
and Sofia are models of women who from their first appearance in the novel are already liberated in their thoughts, attitudes, and behaviors. Other characters, such as Celie, Nettie,
Tashi, Olivia, and Mary Agnes, attain liberation gradually
in the course of their experiences. Liberation also is shown
to have its consequences: Sofia pays dearly, in her beatings,
disfigurement, loss of sight in one eye, as well as in the forced
separation from her children; and Shug is rejected by her
family and exploited by men, including Albert and Brady.

The story uses incest both to dramatize male attempts
to subordinate women and also to propose alternatives to
this subordination. Attempts at subordination take a variety
of forms: not only incest, sexual objectification, and direct
physical violence, but also silencing women and discredit-

ing their voices. An important part of the socialization of males is to promote their voice and words and to discredit or silence the voices of women. Pa, in his effort to "sell" Celie as a fit wife for Mr._____, emphasizes, as his final description of her qualities, that "she tell lies" (18). This whole narrative may be therefore be considered as validating a woman's voice and word in opposition to the words and voices of men.

However, the story also proposes alternatives to the absolute authority of males. Through the representation of female characters in the novel, resistance to this system is most clearly illustrated. Women characters in the novel time and again demonstrate mutual support against male oppression. Celie extends support to her young sister, Nettie, who has been supporting her emotionally all along. Celie willingly submits to violation to protect Nettie from being violated as she was:

> I ast him to take me instead of Nettie while our new mammy sick. But he just ast me what I'm talking about. I tell him I can fix myself up for him. I duck into my room and come out wearing horsehair, feathers, and a pair of our new mammy high heel shoes. He beat me for dressing trampy but he do it to me anyway. (17)

Unlike many incest victims, Celie often has a female protector, a mentor, and a coach, someone who affirms her self-worth. Initially her sister, Nettie, exercises this function. Later in her life, it is Shug. Only during the period when Nettie leaves and before Shug appears is Celie alone and without support, and even then she finds support in an unusual place—from Albert's own sister. Kate, who forces her brother to buy clothes for Celie, goes with her to the store and helps her choose her first store-bought dress (28). She tries to instill in Celie the need for resistance to male domination: "You got to fight them, Celie, she say. I can't do it for you. You got to fight them for yourself" (29). Shug protects Celie against Albert's abuse: "I won't leave, she say, until I know Albert won't even think about beating you" (77). These instances of support suggest that solidarity among women may be the most potent element in disrupting the patriarchal system.

Oppressed and victimized as she is, Celie demonstrates her fundamental resistance to the patriarchal system, in her rejection of males as objects of interest and in her preference for females: "I don't even look at mens. That's the truth. I look at women, tho, cause I'm not scared of them" (15). This preference is expressed even more forcefully the first time she sees Shug's naked body: "First time I got the full sight of Shug Avery long black body with it black plum nipples, look like her mouth, I thought I had turned into a man" (53). This sexual preference, while it may be regarded in part as a reaction to the male abuse she has endured, does indicate that Celie represents an alternative to the role prescribed for women in this male-dominated society.

Nettie's characterization as a sister from the same back-ground as Celie, but with a different experience—having successfully avoided being incested or raped (with the help of her sister and through her own resistance), having received some formal education, granted access to a different social environment even in the U.S., and afforded the opportunity to travel to and live in Africa—permits the exploration of an alternative and contrasting path to liberation and spiritual fulfillment. Nettie's account of her liberation through "real" education indicates that this liberation comes through the truth she is able to confront in relation to her blackness, by exposure to Harlem and Africa. Similarly, Nettie's revelation to Celie about the truth of the paternity of her children lib-erates Celie as well. Before the revelation, Celie does not feel free even to love her own children: "But it hard to think bout them. I feels shame. More than love, to tell the truth" (138).

Other alternatives to male domination are presented primarily through other strongly drawn women characters (particularly Sofia, Shug, and Mary Agnes), whose experiences, words, and actions, which demonstrate ultimately the ineffectiveness of male attempts at subordination, are given substantial treatment in the narrative.

Sofia is drawn as a character who consistently resists male domination. She refuses to be a subordinate human being, to be subservient to men or to Whites. She pays dearly for her resistance, by initially losing her husband, by losing her eyesight in one eye, being imprisoned, being forced into servitude to the mayor's wife, and being separated from her children. Her husband is frustrated by his inability to control her by physical violence. As Celie explains to Harpo, "Some women can't be beat, I say. Sofia one of them" (66). She is severely beaten when she refuses to work for the Mayor's wife, is slapped by the Mayor, and retaliates:

> They crack her skull, they crack her ribs. They tear
> her nose loose on one side. They blind her in one
> eye. She swole from head to foot. Her tongue the
> size of my arm, it stick out tween her teef like a
> piece of rubber. She can't talk. And she just about
> the color of a egg-plant. (87)

Even at the end, after she is hired to clerk in Celie's store, Sofia defies the authority of the white patriarchal society. Celie reports that "she scare that white man. Anybody else colored he try to call 'em auntie or something. First time he try that with Sofia she ast him which colored man his mama sister marry" (245).

Another illustration of a woman who resists male domination is to be found in Shug Avery, the lover of both Mr._____ and Celie. Shug operates outside of the norms of the patriarchal community, continually frustrating Mr._____'s attempts at control, and exercising her sexual freedom in relationships with both men and women. Even before Celie meets her, Celie invests her with a sense of nobility—"She like a queen to me" (28) — and tries to find a purple dress that would convey that sense of royalty. The preacher presents Shug as the epitome of unacceptability: "He talk about a strumpet in short skirts, smoking cigarettes, drinking gin. Singing for money and taking other women mens. Talk bout slut, hussy, heifer and streetcleaner" (49). Shug becomes Celie's savior, protecting her from being physically abused by Albert. When Celie informs her that "He beat me when you not here" (76), Shug reassures her: "I won't leave, she say, until I know Albert won't even think about beating you" (77). Shug's character is extremely significant: depicted as transgressing the role of social acceptability prescribed for women in male-dominated societies, she provides the explanation of the symbolic significance of the title of the narrative and serves as the principal guide to Celie's developing a new concept of the God of her understanding.

One of the most unexpected women characters to exhibit triumph over male dominance is the character whose apparent timidity is reflected in the sobriquet, Squeak, by which she is called. Like Celie, Mary Agnes (Squeak) is an incest victim. The decision made by her friends that she should be used as a sacrificial lamb to try to save Sofia places her in a position to be sexually abused. She sacrifices herself by being raped by her white uncle. However, this sacrifice results in her standing up to Harpo. When he calls her "Squeak," the narrative notes: "She stand up. My name Mary Agnes, she say" (95). Instead of reinforcing her status as a victim, incest provides her with the motivation to emerge as an assertive woman. This sacrifice of her body enables her to gain a voice and a voice of her own: "6 months after Mary Agnes went to git Sofia out of prison, she begin to sing. First she sing Shug's songs, then she begin to make up songs her own self" (96).

The complexity of gender roles also threatens the system of male dominance. All men and all women in the story do not automatically fit the expected gender roles. In some cases, the role expectations of some men and women are in conflict with their real selves. For instance, Albert later in his life is shown to "clean that house just like a woman" (199). He even confesses his early interest in sewing: "When I was growing up, he said, I use to try to sew along with mama cause that's what she was always doing. But everybody laughed at me. But you know, I liked it" (238). Harpo is described as having feminine characteristics: "His eyes be sad and thoughtful. His face begin to look like a woman face" (35). Sofia points out the difference between them which amounts to a reversal of expected gender roles: "I rather be out in the fields or fooling with the animals. Even chopping wood. But he love cooking and cleaning and doing little things around the house" (63). These reversals of gender role expectations subtly subvert the patriarchal system in which the action of the story is set.

The narrative uses individual characters as well as a principle related to the spiritual philosophy that undergirds the story to undermine male dominance. The story illustrates that love provides the most potent opposition to the patriarchal system that supports and condones incest and other forms of violence against women. Celie, an incest victim, a mother whose children have been taken from her, and a battered wife, grows spiritually and emotionally to the point where she can express feeling right with the world and with her abusive husband because of the common love she and Albert have for Shug: "Then I see myself sitting there quilting tween Shug Avery and Mr. _____. Us three set together gainst Tobias and his fly speck box of chocolate. For the first time in my life, I feel just right" (61). The perceived loss of Shug's love, though socially deprecated because it is lesbian and adulterous, is enough to reunite Celie and Albert in a common suffering. Moreover, this love serves as a conduit for redemption. Guilty of the rape of his wife and the attempted rape of his sister-in-law, Albert emerges through this love as a redeemed man, in contrast to Pa, the incest perpetrator, who is never repentant and never redeemed.

Indeed, the possibility of redemption that can transcend the factor of race is one of the fundamental spiritual messages in the story. This is a novel based on primarily black characters, which privileges their voices and experiences, and which even affirms the beauty of blackness in the description of many of its major characters. Celie, Nettie, Shug, Olivia, Tashi, and even Harpo are all described as "black." The novel, however, indicates that the black community is not monolithic and that within this community classism can be as much a divisive factor as racism, contributing to similar abuses of power. The reason why Albert is not with Shug Avery is because his father did not think Shug was good enough for his son. Yet Albert fathered three children with Shug and married another woman whom he did not love. But race plays an important role in this story. The imbalance of power between Blacks and Whites is mainly responsible for many of the instances of injustice in the novel, from Celie's loss of her father through his lynching and the emotional and economic security that he would have provided, to the direct imposition of white power on Sofia. The story presents white people for the most part as oppressors of black folk, both in the United States and in Africa. The novel is careful, however, to demonstrate the redemption of at least one white character. Eleanor Jane, the daughter of the Mayor and his wife, who were the principal abusers of Sofia, ends up working for Sofia. This rehabilitation of Eleanor Jane sends the message that it is possible for Whites also to be redeemed.

The narration of incest in this story is not restricted to a single spatial and geographical context. The epistolary format implies spatial displacement, between sender and addressee. In this case, the displacement is caused directly by the circumstances of male domination and abuse: Nettie has to leave to escape from being violated by her brother-in-law. Her subsequent move to Africa is determined by the position she occupies in the household of missionaries, coincidentally taking care of the children of her sister, Celie. Nettie's separation from her sister, therefore, serves to justify the correspondence and the very structure of the text.

The geographical displacement fulfills important narrative purposes. It provides a justification for the format of the narrative as well as for aspects of the plot: the concealment and the discovery of the letters constitute an obstacle-problem-mystery element (a staple in story-telling) which is guaranteed to generate interest and create suspense. The geographical separation also allows for the dénouement: the unknotting of the various plot threads (revelation of the identity of Celie's children, revelation of the truth about her real father) and the reconciliation at the end—the literal coming back together of the sisters previously separated by the incest culture. The geographical displacement also permits the introduction of a secondary narrator-letter-writer, Nettie, who can fill in the blanks of the narrative of which the primary narrator, Celie, is not aware and to which she (Celie) has no access. In addition, this spatial displacement allows for an expansion of the relevance of the incest theme and of the symbolic scope of the novel. The geographical and sociocultural context of the novel includes not only the southern United States but also West Africa, and the geographical displacement of the action permits plot elements that are not directly related to the theme of incest.

The moving of the action from the United States to Africa permits the narration to present the idea that the oppression of women is not limited to the United States. Nettie finds that there is a striking similarity in the cultural practice of devaluing women among the Olinka and in the community into which she and Celie are brought up. Just as Celie is denied formal education, Nettie discovers that: "[t]he Olinka do not believe girls should be educated" (144). She is disturbed to discover that "[t]here is a way that the men speak to women that reminds me too much of Pa" (149), which suggests that she sees in a system of uncontrolled patriarchy the potential for incest. Most tellingly, in this West African community, the power that men have over women is absolute: "among the Olinka, the husand has life and death power over the wife. If he accuses one of his wives of witchcraft or infidelity, she can be killed" (153).

At the same time, just as exposure to Shug resulted in the transformation of Celie's notion of God, the geographical displacement allows for the evolution of Nettie's notions of spirituality. After her long indoctrination, at least since adolescence, in a Christian world-view, Nettie is transformed by Africa and her exposure to the thinking, culture, and beliefs of the Olinka people and develops a notion of God that is more pantheistic and curiously close to the idea that Celie acquires:

> God is different to us now, after all these years in Africa. More spirit than ever before, and more internal. Most people think he has to look like something or someone—a roofleaf or Christ— but we don't. And not being tied to what God looks like, frees us. (227)

The expansion of the geographical and sociocultural context of the action through Nettie's African odyssey enables the narrative to explore one important area of interest which is not directly connected to incest—the historical and cultural connection between African Americans and continental Africans—so as to dispel some of the myths about this relationship. Africa is not at all presented as an ideal cultural location for American Blacks. While some aspects of life and customs there are treated with respect and understanding, other aspects, such as the subordination of women and attitudes toward slavery, are shown to be of questionable value to women and African-heritage Americans. Therefore Nettie informs Celie, and by extension the reader:

> Did you know there were great cities in Africa, greater than Milledgeville or even Atlanta, thousands of years ago? That the Egyptians who built the pyramids and enslaved the Israelites were colored? That Egypt is in Africa? That the Ethiopia we read about in the Bible meant all of Africa?
>
> Well, I read and I read until I thought my eyes would fall out. I read where the Africans sold us because they loved money more than their own sisters and brothers. (123)

Samuel is conscious of the disconnection of African Americans with, and even rejection by, continental Africans: "The Africans don't even *see* us. They don't even recognize us as the brothers and sisters they sold" (210).

The geographical expansion of the action of the novel allows for the privileging of gender rather than race, and of patriarchy rather than white supremacist notions, as the primary and unifying concern of women, whether in the U.S. or in Africa. While in the American social and geographical context Celie learns from Sofia that "White folks is a miracle of affliction" (103), Nettie can reach the startling conclusion that "Africans are very much like white people back home, in that they think they are the center of the universe and that everything that is done is done for them" (155).

The Color Purple attempts to position itself as more than an account of incest and its effect. In concert with its spiritual focus, the novel insists on its didactic function through the importance attached to learning from life's experiences, as Celia listens to the wisdom acquired by two of the pivotal characters in her life, Sofia and Albert. As a courageous and battle-scarred fighter for her rights as a woman and as a black woman, Sofia makes the point that "Everybody learn something in life" (246). The reformed abuser, Albert, can share the insight he has gained about the need to reflect on the "big things" (247) of life. And Albert is given the privilege of explaining the importance of asking the right questions:

> I start to wonder why us need love. Why us suffer. Why us black. Why us men and women. Where do children really come from. It didn't take long to realize I didn't hardly know nothing. And that if you ast yourself why you black or a man or a woman or a bush it don't mean nothing if you don't ast why you here period. (247)

The musings of these characters at the end of the novel extend the significance of the story beyond incest and emphasize the degree to which the story seeks to function as a vehicle for spiritual and philosophical growth.

The Color Purple is undoubtedly an incest story, but it is also in its essence a women's story, one might even say a womanist story, which centers on the plight of black women in the South at a particular period of America's history. In this realistic and at the same time idealized focus on women, the novel oscillates between the "reality" of the oppression of women and the "fantasy" of women's triumph over the conditions of oppression. The realism of the conditions in which Celie grew up, in relation to a certain period and place in American history, is undeniable, and the representation of life among a West African community is similarly realistic. And yet, the narrative contains a persistent strain of fantasy.

Celie's age, fourteen, at the time of the first incest incident marks her as the oldest incest victim of the five fictional accounts and even of the real-life stories reproduced earlier in this book. Close to the marriageable age for young women of that era, this age is above the average age of most incest victims for the beginning of the incestuous molestation. Celie's level of literacy, evident in her lack of schooling and the crude and unsophisticated language she uses, invites the inference that her victimization, the incest perpetrated on her, is a function of the low socioeconomic status of her family background. Such is not the case, however, because she learns later in the novel that her parents are not only loving and caring but financially well-to-do. Therefore, the difference between Celie's present circumstances and her past links her to the fairy-tale tradition of princesses upon whom a spell has been cast by a wicked witch.

The "true" story of Celie's parentage is related ironically in fairy-tale fashion, with the phrase commonly used in that tradition to open the narration: "Once upon a time, there was a well-to-do farmer who owned his own property near town" (160). This style, adopted by Nettie, who serves as the secondary narrator for a story related by Samuel ["This is Samuel's story, almost word for word" (161)] moves this incest story into the dimension of fantasy. With this narration, Celie is further invested with the aura of a fairy-tale princess, whose noble, or at least respectably comfortable, heritage has been usurped by the forces of evil.

The plot includes some highly melodramatic events that underscore the fantastical aspect of the narrative. The description of Corinne's death provides a relevant illustration. Corinne has suspected her husband, Samuel, of being unfaithful and of having fathered Olivia with Nettie. On her deathbed, Corinne miraculously remembers having met Celie in town years ago: "Celie, in the middle of the night she woke up, turned to Samuel and said: I believe. And died anyway" (171).

The dénouement of the plot is perhaps the most fantastical aspect of the narrative. As the primary victim of different forms of sexual, physical, verbal, and emotional abuse, Celie comes into her own and is healed materially, emotionally, and spiritually, without any formal intervention or treatment. As one of the abusers, though not the primary incest perpetrator, Albert is completely rehabilitated to the point where he and Celie, the person he victimized, can sit together sewing on the porch.

The dénouement represents two important elements in the narration of incest: the hope that recovery and rehabilitation are possible for everyone involved, including male perpetrators of abuse against women, and the strong message of the ultimate liberation of women. This story presents an optimistic, hopeful picture of incest. But it does more than that. Incest is presented as a symbol of the unequal power relationships that exist between men and women, of the difficulty of giving voice to the consciousness of the violation endured by women. The narrative proclaims an underlying belief in the power of prayer and in the existence of a deity that is loving toward and protective of the socially downtrodden, particularly women. A core message of this text is that the evil that is incest cannot stand before the power of good and justice—cannot stand before the power of women's acquisition of self-consciousness. This spiritual force, the God that the narrator comes to know, has the capacity to transform hearts and lives, to change abusers into allies, to change the ugly and the rejected into attractive, productive, and useful members of society, and to turn even incest into a catalyst for the spiritual triumph of women.

Chapter Six

INCEST—
DISRUPTING THE
TEXT OF NATURE:
THE BLUEST EYE

ॐ

In the afterword to the 1994 edition of *The Bluest Eye,* Toni Morrison refers to the novel as a "story of female violation" (214), stimulated by her witnessing the evidence of "racial self-loathing" (210) in one of her childhood friends at the start of elementary school. According to Morrison, in this story she was "exploring the social and domestic aggression that could cause a child to literally fall apart" (210). Morrison also expresses the view that "this is a terrible story about things one would rather not know anything about" (213). A writer's analysis of her or his own work, particularly twenty years after the fact, is not necessarily the most reliable perspective. However, Morrison's comments serve to elucidate aspects of the complexity of this story in which the problem of incest and rape is intimately related to other forms of violation, including what Morrison calls the "demonization of an entire race" (210).

Fictional narratives often offer possibilities of redemption and transformation. In presenting alternatives to reality or reconstructions of reality, such stories, particularly those that target the popular fiction market, often seek to reassure the reader that there is reason to be hopeful. This reassurance usually takes the form of an ending in which the problems confronted by the protagonist are either resolved or show signs of a future optimistic outcome. The reader comes away from the story feeling that all is or will be well. *The Bluest Eye* offers no such reassurance. This novel cannot by any stretch of the imagination be considered as light reading. The story is disturbing, horrifying in its descriptions and implications as well as in its visual (typographic) presentation. This highly symbolic narrative presents an essentially literary formulation of a double problematic: telling an incest story and the act of incest itself.

The discussion that follows does not attempt to be a comprehensive analysis of Morrison's novel. Many such wonderful and insightful analyses already exist. This analysis seeks only to examine *The Bluest Eye* in the specific context of the construction of an incest story, in relation to the questions raised by the text about the notion of incest as a disruption of nature, the challenges of narrating incest arising from such a notion, and the significance of the phenomenon of incest itself as it is presented in this narrative.

The title signals the context in which the central experience of incest and its effects evolve. The superlative indicates not just comparison but a competitive desire for perfection. However, such a desire is usually a mask for dissatisfaction, discontent, and inadequacy. The idea of blue eyes is inevitably related to markers of racial superiority (beauty and perfection) which are entrenched in the sociocultural consciousness of the United States. Therefore, as explored in this narrative, incest is shown through the title to be linked to "race" in the United States. Furthermore, incest in the black community cannot be related without exploring the broader socioeconomic conditions in which such a disruption of nature occurs.

Signifying the totality of forces and processes that control the phenomena of the physical world and all living things, nature may be considered the frame within which all human social and sensorial activities take place. This notion of nature is one of the fundamental underpinnings of the form and content of *The Bluest Eye* and incest is presented as a deformation or disruption of the natural order. The idea that incest may be considered a perversion or disruption of nature is represented symbolically in the organization of the narrative. The division of the text into "Autumn" (7-58), "Winter" (59-93), "Spring" (95-183), and "Summer" (185-206) provides the framework of the natural progression of seasons in which the social life of human beings operates and forms an ironic counterpoint to the variety of "unnatural" occurrences, with Pecola's incest being central, around which the plot of the novel is constructed. Significant plot events are linked specifically to the seasonal divisions of the narrative: Pecola is raped by her father at end of spring section; Frieda is also molested in spring; and the seeds are planted in summer. The importance of this frame is underscored by the fact that it is the belief that young Claudia, the first and principal narrator, holds in the processes of nature which affects her narrative perspective and her interpretation of the events she witnesses.

From the beginning, the narrative hints at the powerlessness of the narrator to change a "natural" process—to make marigolds grow (5). As narrator, Claudia establishes an explicit link between Pecola's incestuous victimization and what appears to be a disruption of natural growth: "We thought, at the time, that it was because Pecola was having her father's baby that the marigolds did not grow" (5). Furthermore, the expression "plot of black dirt" (6), used to describe Pecola metaphorically as well as to indicate the literal depository of the seeds planted by Claudia and Frieda, underscores the link between incest and race as disruptions of nature. Therefore, incest is presented, not only as a social malaise but even more importantly of a deformation as nature, much as is race in the U.S, manifested in the ideology of white supremacy, in the devaluation of African-heritage Blacks and blackness, and in the internalization of white values of beauty by Blacks themselves. Incest and race are thus inextricably intertwined in this narrative.

Many of the characters in this novel are identified in relation to the way in which they are perceived in the context of a presumed "natural" order underlying the community's expectations and are presented in terms that explicitly reference nature or which suggest deviation from or deformation of nature. For instance, Maureen Peal is described as a "disrupter of seasons," in part because she does not conform to the stereotype of blackness since she is both "high-yellow" and rich. Her physical description is conducted in terms that reference the seasons of nature, thereby echoing and underscoring the primary structural divisions in the narrative: "There was a hint of spring in her sloe green eyes, something summery in her complexion and a rich autumn ripeness in her walk" (62).

A similar natural disruption is evident in the socialization of Geraldine, Junior's mother, and the relationship between her and her son. She is presented as one of a group of black women who have learned "how to get rid of the funkiness. The dreadful funkiness of passion, the funkiness of nature, the funkiness of the wide range of human emotions" (83), all stereotypically associated with black people in the United States. The deformation that Geraldine manages to accomplish manifests itself in the resultant perversion of her role as mother, since she abuses her son emotionally by lavishing her affections on her cat rather than on him, who becomes aware of "the difference in his mother's behavior to himself and the cat" (86). This disruption of family relationships that are often considered as natural results in a further deviation: Junior's hatred of his mother and his transference of this hatred to the cat (86).

Deviation from the natural is an essential component of the character of Pauline who presents concrete signs of physical deformity: she is distinguished by a decaying front tooth which she eventually loses, and by the deformity of a crooked foot, the result of a puncture by a rusty nail when she was only in her second year (110), and to which she could attribute her feelings of "separateness and unworthiness" (111). Pauline is also shown to be someone who, like Geraldine, in her desire to be something she was not by virtue of her race and socioeconomic situation, perverts the natural development of her children, including Pecola:

> Them she bent toward respectability, and in so doing taught them fear: fear of being clumsy, fear of being like their father, fear of not being loved by God, fear of madness like Cholly's mother's. Into her son she beat a loud desire to run away, and into her daughter she beat a fear of growing up, fear of other people, fear of life. (128)

Pauline succeeds in transforming Pecola into an excellent candidate for incest and other forms of abuse.

Cholly is presented as suffering a number of disruptions of the natural course of life. He was abandoned by his mother and placed on a junk heap by the railroad when he was only four days old (132). The death of his primary caretaker, Aunt Jimmy, only adds to his feelings of abandonment. He is not only abandoned by his father but rejected by him in the cruelest manner imaginable when he later tracks him down in Macon: "[G]et the fuck outta my face" (156). The disruption of a "natural" childhood experience, in Cholly's being forced by white men with a flashlight to have sex with a girl as they watched him, is used to explain the development in Cholly of a perverted attitude to Whites and to women: "For some reason, Cholly had not hated the white men; he hated, despised, the girl. Even a half-remembrance of this episode, along with myriad other humiliations, defeats, and emasculations, could stir him into flights of depravity that surprised himself" (43). Cholly's experience with Darlene and the white men results in a displacement of anger similar to that manifested by Junior: "Never once did he consider directing his hatred toward the hunters. Such an emotion would have destroyed him. They were big, white, armed men. He was small, black, helpless" (51). Moreover, like many incest perpetrators, Cholly abuses alcohol. We learn that by the time he meets Pauline, as a result of his experiences of rejection, abandonment, and humiliation, he has already become someone with "nothing more to lose" (160), using alcohol to medicate his feelings: "Only in drink was there some break, some floodlight, and when that closed, there was oblivion" (160). Even the young Claudia is aware that "Cholly's always drunk" (102). The first rape of Pecola is perpetrated by him after he staggers home "reeling drunk" (161).

The pedophile Soaphead Church is in many respects a deviation from the norm even of black manhood. He is of mixed blood, from a maternal strain who, similar to Geraldine and her desire to rid herself of black funkiness, learned "to separate herself in body, mind, and spirit from all that suggested Africa" (167). His deviance is also reflected in the fact that his family manifested evidence of what seemed to be a genetic flaw, in its attempt to maintain whiteness through inter-marriage (168). Moreover, his mother, was half-Chinese and died soon after giving birth to him. He was someone who suffered from an "invincible melancholy" (170), equating lovemaking with "communion and the Holy Grail" (170). The narration makes it clear that the eventual desertion by his wife, Velma, and his performing unnatural acts of deviance upon children were predictable, in light of all his unnatural experiences and tendencies.

If nature may be used to signify roles and relationships often expected to obtain between parent and child and between children and their community, Pecola may be considered a character whose deviation from the norm offers an ironic parallel to that of the incest perpetrator, in the multiple rejections and humiliations she suffers at home, at school, and in the wider community and which echo Cholly's experience. Pecola is mistreated at school, "ignored or despised at school, by teachers and classmates alike. She was the only member of her class who sat alone at a double desk" (45). She is ignored and unseen by Mr. Yacobowski, the white shopkeeper: "He does not see her, because for him there is nothing to see" (48). She uses candy, just as Cholly uses alcohol, to medicate the pain of her multiple humiliations and rejections: "What to do before the tears come. She remembers the Mary Janes … She eats the candy, and its sweetness is good.… Three pennies had bought her nine lovely orgasms with Mary Jane" (50). The prostitutes, Miss Marie, China, and Poland, are the only adults in the community to show acceptance and affection to Pecola, but their love for Pecola is not enough to counteract the effects of the rejection, abuse, and rape she endures from other members of her family and community.

The clearest evidence of the degree of Pecola's deviance, however, is her unconcealed obsession with blue eyes. This aberration cannot be separated from other factors that have contributed to her insanity: her deprivation of parental love, compounded by other societal rejections and by the literally mind-bending experience of being raped and impregnated by her own father. The story implies that love, particularly parental love, is natural and all children want and need to experience it for them to develop along "natural" lines. Pecola's tragic deformation begins in the area of love. As she enters the world of womanhood with her first experience of menstruation, Pecola learns that she now has access to motherhood, which her friends, Frieda and Claudia, tell her depends on getting someone to love you. She poses the question to which nobody can provide an answer: "how do you get somebody to love you?" (32). She is haunted by the questions for which her own family provides no answer: "What did love feel like? She wondered. How do grown-ups act when they love each other?" (57). These questions point to the fundamental disruption from which Pecola suffers. Neither her immediate family nor the wider community has provided her with a yardstick by which love, presumed to be natural, can be measured.

The frame of nature within which the action of the story evolves presents a variety of challenges related to both the form and the content of the novel. That incest is characterized by an aura of secrecy and by a taboo that discourages disclosure is already a commonplace. The first word of the prologue to the story, "Quiet" (5), hints at this fundamental attribute of the incest system. The symbolic significance of silence is further underlined by the repetition of the same term at the beginning of Claudia's narration of the exegesis in 1941 (9). The repetition of this term and its usage as part of the black vernacular emphasizes both that this silence as a cultural norm for Blacks and also that what has been kept silent is the black voice. Both the form and the content of *The Bluest Eye* confront the implications of this silence.

Therefore, the narrative challenge is to break through this silence, since the incest that forms the core of this story has not hitherto been addressed narratively and has not been talked about, certainly not in relation to the complexity of factors involved in the victimization of a little black girl. Pecola reveals that when she told her mother about the first rape—"I did tell her" (200)—she was apparently beaten: "They say the way her mama beat her she lucky to be alive herself" (189). Her mother's reaction to being told resulted in Pecola's silence about the second rape that occurred when she was reading on the couch:

> She didn't even believe me when I told her.
> *So that's why you didn't tell her about the second time?*
> She wouldn't have believed me then either. (200)

By its visual and plot structure, the text appears to evolve as a response to a fundamental question: How does one tell a story of incest in the Black American community? The importance of this "how" is explicitly signaled at the end of the opening section which serves as a prologue. The narrator indicates that the narrative is a vehicle for exploring the "how" of the situation as a way of explaining the more difficult "why": "There is really … how" (6). The answer to that "how" question involves the exploration at the narrative level of two further questions: 1) What is the primary formal model for story-telling offered to American Blacks? And 2) What problems arise from this model for the narration of a black experience?

The model used in and by this incest story is that of the (white) reading primer, presenting the story of Jane and her family, which is given an important structural and symbolic role throughout this text. The presentation of the primer narrative suggests right from the beginning of *The Bluest Eye* the danger and potential unreliability of narrative. The opening moves from clear, short, simple sentences, with appropriate punctuation marks, and with all the persons (proper nouns) identified by upper-case first letters [Mother—Jane (3)] in the first paragraph, to a second paragraph in which the same text is reproduced but in which the punctuation disappears as well as the differentiation between proper and common nouns, to a third paragraph repeating the same text, in which the convention of textual differentiation is completely disrupted with no separation between individual words.

While the bundling of words, depriving them of the conventional separation by the removal of spaces, decreases intelligibility, the use of the segments of the primer text serves paradoxically, through their apparent incoherence, to enhance the coherence of the overall narrative. Thus the primer text, deceptive as it may be, is used to mark logical divisions in the arrangement of the story and at the same time to signal the ways in which this incest story deviates from the idealistic model proposed by the primer. The primer text continues to be used epigraphically throughout *The Bluest Eye*: HEREISTHE HOUSE... (33) introduces the Breedloves' house that differs strikingly from that of the Jane family; HEREISTHE FAMILY... (38) presents a description of the Breedloves as a family; SEETHECAT... (81) introduces the incident with Geraldine and Louis Jr.'s cat; SEEMOTHER... (110) introduces us to Pauline Williams; SEEFATHER... (132) introduces the section that focuses on Cholly; SEETHEDOG... (164) introduces the incident with Soaphead, Pecola, and the dog; and LOOKHERE-COMESAFRIEND... (193) presents the dialogue between Pecola and her alternate personality.

The printed text of *The Bluest Eye* graphically suggests that the school primer is a problematic model for Blacks. The apparent simplicity of the primer inscribed in this incest story as a manual for young readers is paradoxically difficult to apprehend and degenerates into unintelligibility. The white primer text, which is literally a primary model for reading, and an introduction to cultural normality, representing a simplistic ideal of American family life (Mother, Father, Dick, Jane), degenerates into a text that is confusing, distorted, and unreadable when conventions of typography are deliberately transgressed. This text and the reality it symbolizes are shown to be misleading, deceptive, and ultimately harmful. Clearly, the primer narrative of Jane and her family has nothing in common with the experience of Pecola and her family.

Narrating incest in the black community requires acknowledging the uselessness and rejection of the white narrative model by employing a narrative voice that is not corrupted by that model. Therefore, as the victim of incest who has internalized white values of perception and beauty to the point of insanity, Pecola is not and cannot be the primary narrator of the story. The text employs a variety of narrative voices that can provide different perspectives on what is essentially the same story with its overlapping contexts: the indoctrination into narrating whiteness through the primer; the need to question belief in the validity of nature as a reliable guide for human behavior; and the influence exercised by environmental factors and experiences. The narration moves smoothly between a variety of first- and third-person narrators. Different first-person narrators are given the opportunity to tell their own story without (authorial or other) editorial comment. Each voice is validated. There is no single authoritative narrator.

The problematic of telling an incest story is explored through the varieties of narrative strategies employed: multiple narrators, first- and third-person, and multiple typographic representations. The multiplicity of narrative perspectives suggests the difficulty of talking about or reporting on incest, even within the fictional genre. One of the fundamental questions raised by this narrative is: Who can tell the incest story? Several possible perspectives are presented in this novel: the independent observer, sympathetic, not objective, but not directly involved; the male perpetrators; the wife and mother; the victim; and the third-person narrative persona who can be used to substitute for and validate any and all of these perspectives.

The primary first-person narrator is Claudia, but she is not sufficiently experienced or knowledgeable to relate this incest story in all its complexity. Hers is an autobiographical story, the coming of age of a young narrator, which frames the story of Pecola's incest and its aftermath, particularly in relation to its significance for her (Claudia). Pecola's story frames three flashbacks in which the stories of Pauline (115-131), Cholly (42, 132-50), and Soaphead Church (177-82) are related.

Claudia's account is supplemented by that of a third-person narrator who provides a perspective (historical) and information of which Claudia is either unaware or incapable, because of her inexperience and age (33-37, 38-44, 81-93, 110-129, 132-163, 164-184). This narrator assumes responsibility for the description of the Breedloves' house (33-58), providing insight into the powerlessness and hopelessness that it reflected: "The only living thing in the Breedloves' house was the coal stove ... The fire seemed to live, go down or die according to its own schemata. In the morning, however, it always saw fit to die" (37). This narrator describes what the Breedlove household was like, the fighting between Cholly and Mrs. Breedlove and the place of Pecola in this family setting, dominated by the conviction of their ugliness. This narrator explains Pecola's obsession with blue eyes as a solution to the problems of her daily life: "Each night, without fail, she prayed for blue eyes" (46).

The third-person narrator is used also to provide perspective on Geraldine and her son, Louis, Junior, who because of their internalized self-hatred and their awareness of "the difference between colored people and niggers" (87), are responsible for humiliating Pecola and kicking her out of their house, calling her "You nasty little black bitch" (92). This same narrator provides background to Pauline Williams 110-131), but this third-person narrative encapsulates segments of the first-person narrative of Pauline herself, whose voice is rendered in italics (112, 115, 117, 118-121, 123-126, 129-131).

The disruption of a narrative convention is indicated by the inscription of the terminology of fairy-tale narration. The third-person narrative of Soaphead Church is introduced in a consciously ironic fashion with the expression "Once there was an old man..." (164) which echoes and mocks at the conventional opening of (Western ?) fairy tales. The irony of this narration is enhanced by the description of Soaphead, a pedophile with a preference for little girls, as a "clean old man" (167). This third-person narration is interrupted by Soaphead's letter to God, which functions as a first-person narrative (177-182). In Soaphead's letter, as he reflects upon his past life, he employs the phrase "Once upon a time," (172) which once again ironically echoes the fairly-tale aspect of the third-person narration of his life.

Typography is an important aspect of any scripted/ printed narrative, and *The Bluest Eye* devotes a lot of attention to the manipulation of different typographical formats. Even though the narrative manifests some of the characteristics of oral story-telling, particularly in the fidelity of its representation of voice, in narration and in dialogue, the text is self-consciously scripted and profoundly autoreferential, in that it plays with, and departs from, typographical and even oral conventions of narration.

One convention that is used to distinguish narrative voices is that of page justification. Full justification is linked to third-person narration that is employed by an apparently more objective and more knowledgeable narrative persona who recalls events that would fall outside Claudia's frame of knowledge or experience. Thus, the sections narrated by the third-person narrator are fully justified—right as well as left (33-58, 81- 93, 110-183)— and suggest the formality of adherence to the convention of printed narrative. However, the convention of typographical justification is disrupted in the first-person, more informal, narrative by Claudia (9-32, 61-80, 97-109, and 187-192) which is not right justified, but it is clearly Claudia's persona who relates in the first person the typographically justified segment (204-206) with which the novel ends, when presumably Claudia has acquired the authority with which this more formal format is invested. Informal and non-authoritative, Pauline's first-person narrative (112, 115, 117, 118-121, 123-126, and 129-131) is also unjustified and is presented in italics, just as italics are used right at the beginning in the prologue of the narrative for Claudia's first-person commentary. In the dialogue between two Pecola personas, one persona is differentiated by the use of italics (193-204). Soaphead's letter to God (176-182), which is a first-person communication, is fully justified unlike the other first-person narrative segments. These typographical variations not only undermine the conventions of printed narrative, but in so doing also signal the multiple challenges involved in the telling of this incest story.

These challenges are reflected not only in the formal structure and presentation of *The Bluest Eye* but also in its content. Incest is not treated in *The Bluest Eye* as a generalized experience but in a specific, though broad, context: the socioeconomic and ideological conditions that characterize black life as American Blacks move in the post-Reconstruction period from the south to the north. The incest presented in this novel is carefully contextualized, as is that in Alice Walker's *The Color Purple*: incest perpetrated by a black man on his black daughter in a black household at a certain period of American socioeconomic history. Incest in this context is supplemented by other forms of abuse which are endemic in this community: the abuse of racist indoctrination into the ideology of white supremacy; abuse of women; the sexual abuse of children (Frieda by Mr. Henry; girls by Soaphead); and all black society by socioeconomic conditions. Hence, the racial characteristics and socioeconomic background of the characters implicated or involved in the community in which the incest takes place have to form part of the narrative.

The incest system in this story is connected to the community's and indeed the larger American society's system of value in relation to race. Claudia learns from an early age that "Adults, older girls, shops, magazines, newspapers, window signs—all the world had agreed that a blue-eyed, yellow-haired, pink-skinned doll was what every girl child treasured" (20). The power of this socialization is such that even she, who initially resists to the point of destroying white baby dolls (22), eventually learns to worship Shirley Temple (23). The peers of Claudia and Pecola manifest the damage caused by this socialization into privileging whiteness. The abuse by the group of boys from Pecola's school is attributed by the narrator to "their contempt for their own blackness" and "their exquisitely learned self-hatred, their elaborately disguised hopelessness" (65). Because of the ideological context which determines Pecola's beliefs and experiences, incest in her case is more than a single act perpetrated by an individual. Indeed, Pecola is abused over and over again. She is abused by and through the responsible adults at home and at school. She is also abused by the U.S.A in which she unconsciously believes and which functions for her as a super parent, but which privileges and promotes white standards of beauty and personhood. The fundamental betrayal, the fundamental violation, is by the value system and the ideology, intrinsically American, to which she subscribes.

The fragmentation of Pecola's personality which occurs may be attributed as much to the violent experience of incest (the rape by her father) as to the violence of the ideology of self-worthlessness to which she subscribes—an ideology reinforced by the treatment she receives in relation to her condition as a little black girl at the hands of Whites in her community and of her own mother. Mr. Yacobowski's reaction to her forms part of the violence of nonrecognition and of nonpersonhood associated with the condition of being black: "Yet this vacuum is not new to her. It has an edge; somewhere in the bottom lid is the distaste. She has seen it lurking in the eyes of all white people. So the distaste must be for her, her blackness"(49). This belief is responsible for the conviction of needing blue eyes in order to be okay—the conviction of her ugliness and unworthiness which, in her mind, only blue eyes could counteract. Indeed, the yearning by a little black girl for the blue eyes of a little white girl is shown at the end to be an extremely traumatic natural disruption: "the horror at the heart of her yearning is exceeded only by the evil of fulfillment" (204).

Incest in this story is presented in its relation to both the ideological and the socioeconomic situation of the Blacks that form part of the community. For this reason the narrative specifies that Cholly is a "renting black" (18), to be distinguished from "propertied black people [who] spent all their energies, all their love, on their nests" (18). Furthermore, the narrator presents the ironically named Breedloves as people who had internalized and were convinced of their own ugliness: "It was as though some mysterious all-knowing master had given each a cloak of ugliness to wear, and they had each accepted it without question" (39).

The sense of powerlessness associated with the condition of Blacks is shown to be a contributory factor in the perpetration of child molestation, so that for both of the primary molesters in this narrative, Cholly and Soaphead, child molestation is an outlet for the exercise of the power they cannot otherwise exert and for the perversion of the very concept of love occasioned by their social experience. Child molestation is in both cases a manifestation of misdirected violence and perverted love. Consequently, the narration focuses on the emotional complexity that arises from this misdirection of frustrated control and emotion.

The description of Pecola's incest experience highlights the complexity of the factors involved in this act of violence perpetrated by a father on his daughter. The third-person narration specifies the time of year in which the act takes place: spring, stereotypically and ironically associated with burgeoning love. The narration also focuses on the perpetrator, Cholly, on his emotions and perceptions, rather than on those of his daughter. In fact, she is presented through his eyes. This perspective radically affects the reader's view of incest and manipulates the reader into a form of complicity with the perpetrator, since his perceptions are validated in the very process of narration. His reactions and actions are not justified, but they are explained and presented in a context of apparent rationality. The details provided by the narrator serve to emphasize his humanity: "Cholly saw her dimly and could not tell what he saw or what he felt. Then he became aware that he was uncomfortable; next he felt the discomfort dissolve into pleasure. The sequence of his emotions was revulsion, guilt, pity, then love" (161). The focus on the humanity of the perpetrator introduces a dimension rarely seen in incest narratives. This focus militates against facile judgment or rejection of Cholly as simply a morally reprehensible person. The details presented earlier about his background and childhood experiences force the reader to acknowledge that Cholly is also a victim of abuse and that the American ideological conditioning has contributed to the psychic damage and mental and emotional confusion from which he still suffers and which expresses itself in the violation of his daughter. This scene invites speculation on the combination of violence, the imposition of power, and the instinct for sexual gratification as an outlet for perverted love, which comprises the act of incest.

The narration resists dismissing Cholly simply as "bad" because he is an incest perpetrator. Part of the story to be told is the complex of motivations and emotions that even such a reprehensible character experiences. The narrator emphasizes the contradictions in Cholly's emotional reaction to Pecola: "He wanted to break her neck —but tenderly. Guilt and impotence rose in a bilious duet" (161). His mental and emotional confusion is conveyed through a series of questions, as the third-person narrator enters into Cholly's consciousness: "What could he do for her—ever? What give her? What say to her? What could a burned-out black man say to the hunched back of his eleven-year-old daughter?" (161). The description of Cholly in this final question extends the significance and causation of incest in this case beyond an act perpetrated by Cholly as an individual to the wider social circumstances which have formed him and by which he is defined. The narration avoids judgmental commentary and focuses only on detailing the process by which Cholly's mental and emotional confusion develops, as a gesture by Pecola, standing "on one foot scratching the back of her calf with her toe" (162), disorients him further, as he recalls "that was what Pauline was doing the first time he saw her in Kentucky" (162). The narrator is able to explain the awakening of sexual desire, which is directed not toward Pecola, but toward Pauline: "The confused mixture of his memories of Pauline and the doing of a wild and forbidden thing excited him, and a bolt of desire ran down his genitals" (162). The narrator uses key terms to indicate Cholly's welter of contradictory emotions: "lust," "politeness," "fuck," "tenderness," "hatred" (162-3). Only in the final short paragraph of the scene and chapter does the narrator transfer attention to Pecola: "So when the child regained consciousness, she was lying on the kitchen floor under a heavy quilt, trying to connect the pain between her legs with the face of her mother looming over her" (163).

The story involves relating the similar emotional confusion that characterizes Soaphead's abuse of Pecola. Soaphead's reaction to Pecola as he prepares to abuse her ["A surge of love and understanding swept through him, but was quickly replaced by anger. Anger that he was powerless to help her" (174)] echoes that of Cholly earlier: "What could he do for her—ever? ....If he looked into her face, he would see those haunted, loving eyes. The hauntedness would irritate him—the love would move him to fury" (161). The abuse of a helpless child by both Cholly and Soaphead is related to their awareness of their own powerlessness in relation to society as a whole. And this aspect of the abuse forms an essential element in the story to be told.

Yet the story is as much that of the perpetrators as of the victims. It is the story of individuals like Cholly, Soaphead, and Mr. Henry, who attempt to exercise power over the powerless by sexually molesting presumably helpless children like Pecola and Frieda. But the story is not limited to that of the perpetrators. Since the perpetrators operate within a specific community with its own attitudes and values, the story has to explore as well the ways in which the members of the community respond to both perpetrators and victims.

The response of members of the community in each case of sexual molestation or attempted sexual molestation is an indicator of the extent to which the victim or the perpetrator is protected by the community and by the family unit. This factor is at the root of the marked difference between Mr. Henry's sexual molestation of Frieda and Pecola's incest. The community, of which young Claudia may be considered a representative, is certainly aware that Mr. Henry kept "girlie magazines" (26) in his room. While this fact by itself may not have been predictive of sexually deviant behavior, it does foreshadow his later attempt at molestation. In Frieda's case, she has parents to whom she can disclose the molestation. Not only is she immediately believed, but both of her parents take action: her father throws a tricycle at Mr. Henry's head and knocks him off the porch; her mother hits him with a broom; her father gets a gun and shoots at him (100).

The contrast in the family situation of Frieda and Pecola is rendered even more striking when the children visit Mrs. Breedlove at her place of work and Pecola accidentally spills a pan of blueberry cobbler. Abusing her daughter verbally and kicking her out of the house while comforting the "little girl in pink" (109), Pecola's mother's reaction speaks not only to Pecola's lack of a protective maternal mantle but also to her lack of human value as a black girl even in her mother's eyes. Also revealed is that Pecola's disclosure to her mother results in her not being believed and even in being beaten. The community and Pecola's mother's exhibit similar reactions to her of rejection and even of condemnation. The community's reaction to Pecola's rape is recounted through a series of unedited comments overheard by Claudia as narrator, including the support expressed for Pecola's being asked to be taken out of school because "She carry some of the blame" (189), even though she was only twelve years old. Claudia also notes that nobody in the community seems to share the sorrow she felt for Pecola: "And I believe our sorrow was the more intense because nobody else seemed to share it" (190). Therefore, the tragedy of the whole story is not simply the incest perpetrated on Pecola by Cholly and its traumatic aftermath but from the perspective of the more socially conscious narrator the complicity of the community in her abuse, degradation, and fragmentation.

As a fictional incest story, *The Bluest Eye* contains a number of features that correlate with the reality reported in of non-fictional accounts. The characteristics of the perpetrator's partner, her low self-esteem, her lack of nurturing of her child, the distance she exhibits toward her daughter, and her disbelief of her child when told of the incest are all typical of the "silent partner" of the abuse perpetrator. Pecola's reaction to her mother in deciding not to tell about the second rape is equally typical. Similarly, alcohol abuse, such as that reported as characteristic of Cholly, has been well documented as a typical factor in rape and sexual molestation.

Yet *The Bluest Eye* differs significantly from most fictional or factual accounts of incest in several ways. The visual text itself that offers itself to the reader disrupts the convention of typescripted narrative. The typography hints at abnormality. The different typographic formats used indicate directly the relative readability and intelligibility of texts. The suggestions of textual incoherence implicit in the typographical format of *The Bluest Eye* invite speculation on the degree to which any coherent narrative is trustworthy.

The narrative is also different and disturbing in the depiction of characters such as Cholly and Soaphead Church, the most strongly drawn black male figures in the novel. Their characterization invites reflection on the extent to which the aberration that both of them manifest (violence and sexual deviance) may be regarded as typical of black males. Indeed, incest in this story may be read as a metaphor for the situation of Blacks in the U.S.A. *The Bluest Eye* posits the paradox of absolute liberty—freedom without responsibility or morality—the condition reached by Cholly (and stereotypically dreamed of by American Blacks) in response to the multiple rejections and abuses he has endured. It is precisely this liberty that leads to a deformation of the very concept of love and becomes therefore dangerous.

What is radically different about this narrative is that at least two of the principal abusers, as well as the mother, are allowed to tell their own stories. In most incest stories, both fictional and non fictional, the focus is usually on the perspectives and voices of the victims, who are allowed to judge and mediate responses to the perpetrators. In *The Bluest Eye* this convention is completely disrupted. Not only is the primary victim not the principal narrator, but the characteristics, perspectives, and experiences of Cholly, Soaphead, Pauline and even Geraldine are given full and respectful treatment. This exposure to the abusers brings a fresh perspective to the story and obliges the reader to participate in the attribution of responsibility.

The Bluest Eye places the incest story in a perspective rarely shown in factual or fictional accounts, particularly in the conclusion the narrator reaches:

> This soil is bad for certain kinds of flowers. Certain seeds it will not nurture, certain fruit it will not bear, and when the land kills of its own volition, we acquiesce and say the victim has no right to live. We are wrong, of course, but it doesn't matter. It's too late. (206)

With reference to the plot of the novel, the multiple victimizations of Pecola and of other characters are emotionally unsettling. There is no happy ending, no suggestion of rehabilitation, reconciliation, or redemption. Most strikingly, the victim never recovers from the trauma. Indeed, this is the only incest story among those fictional and non-fictional treated here that presents a victim who does not survive. At the end of the story, Pecola is a broken individual, ostracized by the community. The fracture of her personality is clearly demonstrated by the internal dialogue of two distinct personas. This outcome is more in tune with reality, since "recovery" from incest usually requires some form of intervention and professional help and victims who do not have the benefit of therapy tend typically to exhibit and experience different degrees of psychic dislocation. The novel suggests that the fracture caused by incest is irreparable and that the disruption of incest is total and unending.

The Bluest Eye is only tangentially an incest story. The title suggests the central importance of racism. The story is as much about racism in America as it is about incest. Pecola is shattered as much, or perhaps more, by western standards of beauty as she is by being raped by her father. The effect of the incest on Pecola is undeniably traumatic. However, that direct and indirect instances of racism fuel her low self-esteem and make her weak and vulnerable are similarly undeniable. The connection between incest and racism is evident in that her being raped by her father convinces her that her ugliness is beyond repair and leads her to madness.

After the incest, Pecola asks for blue eyes. Therefore, incest in *The Bluest Eye* cannot be separated from race and is used as a metaphor for the experience of Blacks in the United States. Morrison's novel suggests that incest is as much a disruption of the natural order as is race and that constructing and telling an incest story, particularly incest in the black community, require a disruption of the "natural" (i.e. white) order of story-telling. This story is thus profoundly subversive, not only in the account given of the correlation between incest and race and in the narrative techniques it employs, but also in the responsibility it places on the reader. The full story of incest and race finally is told, with all perspectives being represented, and the reader has to confront the degree to which he or she is willing to disrupt the "natural" social order, as this narrative does. With *The Bluest Eye* the incest story is more than an individual tragedy. It becomes an indictment of a whole society.

Afterword

❦

These studies of "factual" and fictional incest narratives highlight intriguing perspectives on the nature of narrative and on the relevance of the incest experience to the production and construction of all narratives. The characteristics of narrative are well known and have been thoroughly theorized, analyzed, and represented: the basic importance of plot and character, fundamental elements of continuity and coherence, manipulations of spatiality and temporality, and the underlying control exercised by narrative perspective. The most fascinating feature in the construction of both "factual" and fictional narratives as explored in the preceding chapters has been the ambiguity of the authorial role. What is absolutely beyond dispute is that the autonomous narrative does not exist. While the elements that can constitute a potential narrative exist independently of narrator or author, a narrative cannot narrate itself automatically. All narratives have to be constructed and mediated.

The incest experience exemplifies and illuminates this paradoxical dynamic. Indeed, the incest experience may be considered as emblematic of the most fundamental aspect of narrative. It represents an unvoiced experience that begs to be narrated, but which, because of the peculiar combination of circumstances surrounding the experience, cannot narrate itself. Because of their perspectives and limitations, the perpetrator and the victim are less than adequate narrators. The warped sensibility of the perpetrator would produce, even in the best of circumstances, only a warped narrative. The trauma suffered by the victim, trapped in any case in a socially imposed mutism, affects the memory, itself at the best of times discontinuous and unreliable, on which the narrative would be based. In both cases, some form of authorial mediation is necessary to construct and produce a coherent narrative.

Paradoxically, other people's incest narratives serve in many cases as mediators for the incest victim's construction of her/his incest narrative. The process of constructing the incest narrative facilitates the movement from victim to survivor. Breaking of the silence, whether orally or on paper, leads to healing. In this respect, narrative is a powerful tool, whether fictional or factual. As the triumph of Precious attests, narratives need to be constructed as a means of helping the incest victim overcome the traumatic effects of the experience, since, as Pecola exemplifies, many victims do not overcome the devastating effects of the experience.

A multiplicity of stories has remained unvoiced. This narrative inhibition is bound to exist even in the formal learning communities of school, college, and university. Given the prevalence of incest, more than likely every class of twenty or more will contain students who have experienced forms of incest or childhood sexual abuse. Therefore, teachers who venture into the territory of teaching narrative construction using incest as a focus or examine texts that feature incest experiences need to be sensitive to the ramifications of incest and its effects and to be prepared to refer students to the therapeutic community if need be. In the classes in which the "Narrating Abuse" course has been taught, the enthusiastic response of all students to the opportunity to participate in the activity of learning how to construct their own fictional narratives has been extremely encouraging. Some students have discovered a talent of which they had been unaware. Some have produced narratives that are well worth publishing. All have delighted in the increased self-knowledge that develops from the process of narrative construction. However, of particular relevance to all teachers is that the practice of narration in the classroom can serve as a safe activity for some incest survivors to construct their own stories and so begin the process of healing.

References

৯৯৯

Bhuvaneswar, Chaya, and Shafer, Audrey. 2004. Survivor of that Time, that Place: Clinical Uses of Violence Survivors' Narratives. *Journal of Medical Humanities* 25.2: 109-27.

Browne, A., & Finkelhor, D. 1986. Impact of Child Sexual Abuse: A Review of the Research. *Psychological Bulletin* 99: 66-77.

Buck, Craig, and Forward, Susan. 1978, 1988. *Betrayal of Innocence: Incest and Its Devastation*. New York: J.P. Tarcher, Inc.; Penguin.

Cebik, L.B. 1986. Understanding Narrative Theory. *History and Theory* 25.4: 58-81.

Hamer, Mary. 2002. *Incest: A New Perspective*. Cambridge: Polity.

Hill, Donna. 2004. *In My Bedroom*. New York: St. Martin's Press.

Howard, George S. 1991. Culture Tales: A Narrative Approach to Thinking, Cross-cultural Psychology, and Psychotherapy. *American Psychologist* 46.3: 187-197.

Hurley, Dorothy L. 1990. Incest and the Development of Alcoholism in Adult Female Survivors. *Alcoholism Treatment Quarterly* 7.2: 41-56.

Hurley, Dorothy L. 1991. Women, Alcohol and Incest: An Analytical Review. *Journal of Studies on Alcohol* 52.3: 253-268.

Hurley, Dorothy L. 2004. Spiritual Impact of Childhood Sexual Abuse: Some Implications for Teacher Education. *Journal of Religion & Abuse* 6.2: 81-101.

Liddell, Janice Lee. 1999. Agents of Pain and Redemption in Sapphire's *Push. Arms Akimbo: Africana Women in Contemporary Literature*. Gainesville: UP of Florida: 135-46.

Miller, Karen E. Quinones. 2002. *I'm Telling*. New York: Simon & Schuster.

Morrison, Toni. 1970, 1994. *The Bluest Eye*. New York: Penguin, Plume.

Polusny, Melissa A., and Victoria M. Follette. 1995. Long-term Correlates of Child Sexual Abuse: Theory and Review of the Empirical Literature. *Applied and Preventive Psychology* 4: 143-166.

Rountree, Wendy A. 2004. Overcoming Violence: Blues Expression in Sapphire's *Push. Atenea* 24.1: 133-143.

Sapphire/ Ramona Lofton. 1996, 1997. *Push*. New York: Random House, Vintage.

Stiles, William B., Lara Honos-Webb, and James A. Lani. 1999. Some Functions of Narrative in the Assimilation of Problematic Experiences. *Journal of Clinical Psychology* 55.10: 1213-1226.

Vogeltanz, Nancy D., Sharon C. Wilsnack, T. Robert Harris, Richard W. Wilsnack, Stephen A. Wonderlich, and Arlinda F. Kristjanson. 1999. Prevalence and Risk Factors for Childhood Sexual Abuse in Women: National Survey Findings. *Child Abuse and Neglect* 23.6: 579-592.

Walker, Alice. 1982. *The Color Purple*. New York: Washington Square Press.

Index

Africa/African 8, 10-13, 16, 20, 48, 52, 53, 84, 100, 119, 133, 137-141, 148, 150

Alcohol/Alcoholic 4, 8, 11, 22, 25, 26, 29, 35-37, 41, 52, 72, 150, 151, 164

Alcoholics Anonymous (AA) 26, 36

Armstrong, L. 8, 9

Ashley 15, 20

Author 1, 2, 7, 12, 15, 20, 21, 64, 109, 112, 118, 119, 169

Betrayal of Innocence 20

Bible 1, 23, 34, 140

Browne, A. 5

Buck, Craig 20

Cebik, I. B. 7

Character/Characterization 1, 3, 6, 7, 11, 48-53, 55-68, 70, 71, 73, 75-78, 80-85, 87, 88, 95-101, 109, 113, 120, 121, 124, 131-137, 141, 148, 149, 151, 152, 157, 158, 161, 162, 164-166, 169

Dénouement 61, 110, 114, 138

Destiny 1, 15, 20

Drink, Drinking 6, 25, 26, 29-31, 35, 36, 41, 135, 150

Drugs 25, 26, 35, 48

Europe/European 10-12, 63

Falls, Cece 66

Farrakhan, Louis 95, 100, 107, 108

Finkelhor, D. 5

First-person (narration) 12, 15, 21, 47, 48, 65, 75, 103, 113, 155, 157, 158

Flashback 40, 47, 56

Follette, Victoria M. 6

Forward, Susan 20

Gabrielle 15, 20, 32

Hamer, Mary 8, 9
Harlem 53, 90, 113, 133
Harlem Renaissance 53
Hill, Donna 16, 63, 66
Howard, George S. 2, 16
Hughes, Langston 53, 95, 113
Hurley, Dorothy L. 1, 4, 8, 9, 11, 12
Hurley, E. Anthony 11, 12

I'm Telling 16, 45, 47, 49, 51, 53, 55, 57-59, 61, 62, 97, 110
In My Bedroom 63-65, 67-69, 71-73, 75-77, 79, 81, 83-86
Islam, Nation of 48, 100, 107

Johnson, James Weldon 53

Kayla 15, 20

Liddell, Janice Lee 88

McKay, Claude 53
Memory 3, 4, 24, 34, 66, 69, 101, 102, 170
Miller, Karen E. Quinones 16, 45, 46
Morrison, Toni 16, 20, 145, 146, 167

Orgasm 1, 40

Patriarchy 9, 11, 114, 126, 127, 139, 140

Perpetrator 5, 48, 57, 59, 63, 74, 75, 77, 85, 96, 103, 124, 129, 130, 131, 137, 143, 151, 161, 163, 164, 170
Plot 1, 46, 52-58, 60-62, 67, 68, 70, 71, 75, 79, 80, 85, 86, 89, 90, 110, 114, 122, 138, 142, 147, 153, 166, 169
Polusny, Melissa A. 6
Polynesia 8
Push 16, 87-89, 91-93, 95, 97, 99, 101-103, 105-107, 109, 111-115, 125

Race, Racism 9, 10, 16, 84, 98, 100, 107, 114, 137, 140, 145, 146, 148, 149, 159, 166, 167
Rape 5, 24, 61, 72, 79, 91, 94-96, 101, 106, 108, 109, 118, 129, 130, 137, 145, 150-153, 159, 164
Rountree, Wendy 88

Sapphire/ Lofton, Ramona 16, 87, 109
Seneca 88
Silence 8-10, 14, 16, 45, 55-57, 70, 83, 104, 105, 120, 123, 132, 152, 153, 170
Sophocles 88
Spielberg, Stephen 117
Stony Brook 13
Suicide 78, 80

Survivor 4, 19, 21, 50, 61,
64-67, 74, 76, 83-87, 89, 94,
103, 113, 170

Taboo 8-10, 12, 14-16, 45, 57,
62, 65, 69, 70, 103, 120, 152
The Bluest Eye 20, 145-147,
149, 151-155, 157-159, 161,
163-167
The Color Purple 16, 113, 114,
117, 119, 121, 123, 125,
127, 129, 131, 133, 135,
137, 139-141, 143, 158
Therapy, Therapeutic 14, 16,
19, 20, 26, 30, 36, 39, 61, 62,
68, 74, 85, 86, 90, 99, 112,
113, 166, 170
Third-person (narration) 2, 47,
48, 65, 68, 69, 72-74, 78, 80,
155-157, 160, 162
Tonga 8

Vogeltanz, Nancy D. 5
Voice 9-12, 15, 20, 21, 28, 48,
49, 51, 56-58, 69, 72-74,
78-82, 86, 88, 102-106, 112,
123, 124, 132, 135, 143,
155 - 157

Walker, Alice 16, 95, 113, 117,
128, 158